THE WORKS OF WILLIAM H. BEVERIDGE

Volume 5

THE LONDON SCHOOL OF ECONOMICS

THE LONDON SCHOOL OF ECONOMICS
And Its Problems 1919-1937

LORD BEVERIDGE

Routledge
Taylor & Francis Group

LONDON AND NEW YORK

First published in 1960

This edition first published in 2015
by Routledge
2 Park Square, Milton Park, Abingdon, Oxon, OX14 4RN

and by Routledge
711 Third Avenue, New York, NY 10017

Routledge is an imprint of the Taylor & Francis Group, an informa business

© 1960 George Allen & Unwin Ltd.

British Library Cataloguing in Publication Data
A catalogue record for this book is available from the British Library

ISBN: 978-1-138-82643-4 (Set)
eISBN: 978-1-315-73730-0 (Set)
ISBN: 978-1-138-82834-6 (Volume 5)
eISBN: 978-1-315-73816-1 (Volume 5)

Publisher's Note
The publisher has gone to great lengths to ensure the quality of this reprint but points out that some imperfections in the original copies may be apparent.

Disclaimer
The publisher has made every effort to trace copyright holders and would welcome correspondence from those they have been unable to trace.

LORD BEVERIDGE

THE LONDON SCHOOL
OF ECONOMICS
AND ITS PROBLEMS
1919-1937

ILLUSTRATED

RUSKIN HOUSE
GEORGE ALLEN & UNWIN LTD
MUSEUM STREET LONDON

FIRST PUBLISHED IN 1960

PRINTED IN GREAT BRITAIN
in 11 on 12 point Georgian type
BY THE BLACKFRIARS PRESS LTD
LEICESTER

PREFACE

THIS book is a sequel to another book written by Janet Beveridge, my wife, that is being published at nearly the same time. Janet's book is called *An Epic of Clare Market* and tells the story of the birth of the London School of Economics and Political Science in 1895 and its development to 1919. My book tells the story of the same School and of the main problems facing it in the eighteen years following, from 1919 to 1937. I became Director of the School in October 1919 and Janet became its Secretary soon after, so that this book is an account of what we did together in the School of Economics. She was then Jessy Mair, her first husband and my cousin and friend David Beveridge Mair living into 1942. She and I were married in December 1942 and she became Janet Beveridge. She was Jessy Mair throughout the period of this book, but I call her Janet throughout unless there is any special reason for using her earlier name.

My Janet naturally continued to be deeply interested, to the end of her life last April, in the School where she had spent so many happy and productive years from 1919 to 1937, and within the past few years she wrote for the journal of the Students' Union of the School, called the *Clare Market Review* a number of articles on her experiences there. I have quoted from her articles freely in this book, as they deserve most eminently, for they are delightful reading. I have kept myself straight on her articles throughout, as she would have wanted me to do so.

The period covered in this book is from 1919 to 1937, but I am writing it, in 1959, about a living institution which has grown and changed continually since I left it. No doubt its more recent history will be put on record before long and I make no attempt to anticipate that record. But, every now and again, I cannot ignore wholly the possibility that what I am writing about the past has no relevance to conditions at the School today. The Commerce Degree, for instance, which was the financial basis of the School's new start in 1919, has disappeared as a separate degree. The changes in the student body which are a main theme of my third chapter have been followed by further changes. The sources from which the School's income comes are relatively quite different today from what they were in my time. The relation to the University of London is probably quite different also.

On some of these points, I have been able to give warning by recourse to statistics. My first visit to the School of Economics, fifty-five years ago, was inspired by anxiety to learn something about statistical method from Professor Bowley. I make no apology, accordingly, for including in this volume an Appendix of Statistics. One of the features of statistics is that, like the School itself, they go on and on. In giving figures of students, teachers, income and so on for my review period 1919-37, I have shown them in relation to what happened earlier and has happened since, by printing comparable figures for two years before World War I and for the latest years of all (1956-8), and by noting differences and similarities as between one time and another.

Every now and again also I have referred to something that is happening today, or to a modification of my own opinions of 1937 or before then. 'This day' or 'today' in my text means 1959. But such references are rare. The purpose of this book is to put 1919-37 on record, as a time of activity and happiness for Janet and myself.

I have covered this period already in an earlier book of autobiographical character called *Power and Influence*. But most of what is dealt with there, including the Bloomsbury Site, my Side-Shows and the Fading of Dreams as World War II approached, falls out of the scope of this book, written as it is in an altogether more personal tone, from new material, and dealing only with the School. I have naturally, from time to time, made quotations from that earlier book or given references to it. I thank the publishers of that book Messrs. Hodder and Stoughton for their kindly consent to these references and quotations.

On July 14, 1959, I gave a Centenary Lecture at the School on Sidney and Beatrice Webb and the School, and I have included the substance of this lecture, as well as a good deal of other matter concerned with the Webbs and their

8

achievement and my varied contacts with them over forty years, in the last chapter of this book.

I acknowledge with deep gratitude the help given to me by the Director, the Secretary and the Librarian of the School and by many others who worked with them, in collecting and studying the material used in this book. I have enjoyed also most welcome help on special subjects from members of the teaching staff. For everything printed in it, whether a statement of fact or an opinion or judgment, I alone am responsible.

I thank the Passfield Trustees for putting at my disposal the letters and documents under their charge which I have used. I have a number of letters received from Sidney or Beatrice or copies of letters written by me to them or about them. When I have finished with this book, I should like to offer all such letters in my possession to the Passfield Trustees for their care.

I thank my step-daughter Elspeth (Mrs. R. S. Burn) for having made yet another Index for me, with unexampled speed.

CONTENTS

PREFACE   *page* 7

   I   A NEW START AFTER WAR   15
  II   THE BATTLE OF HOUGHTON STREET   23
 III   STUDENTS AND THEIR PROBLEMS   30
       The Students Change   30
       The Needs of Students   33
       Students Have Their Problems   40
  IV   TEACHERS AND THEIR PROBLEMS   46
       Teachers Must Live   46
       Teachers Should Research   50
       The Issue of Political Activity   52
   V   ECONOMISTS AT PLAY   59
  VI   PRE-OCCUPATIONS OF A DIRECTOR   65
       Public Service   67
       Social Life   69
       Care of Parents   71
       Motors, Mountains and Manuscripts   73
 VII.   THE PROBLEM OF ACADEMIC SELF-
       GOVERNMENT   78
VIII   THE SCOPE AND METHOD OF SOCIAL
       SCIENCE   83
       Scope of Social Science   83
       The Natural Bases of the Social Sciences   88
       Method of Social Science   94
  IX   CENTENARY OF THE WEBBS   98
       The Webb Achievement   98
       Personal Qualities and Other Factors   100
       My Contacts with the Webbs   103
       Sidney's Favourite Child   106
       Passion for New Ideas   110
APPENDIX I   Statistics   117
APPENDIX II   Resolutions on Staff and Political
         Activities   125
APPENDIX III   Notes on Some of the Illustrations   127
INDEX   129

ILLUSTRATIONS

1. Janet, having just received her O.B.E., with
   her four children   *facing page* 16

2. L.S.E. Rag, May 1920   17

3. Old Houghton Street Houses   32

4. The Army Class 1930-31, outside the old front
   door   33

5. Arnold Plant and Lionel Robbins at Avebury   48

6. Wallas, Ware and Siegfried with others at
   Avebury   49

7. Edwin Cannan, 1920   64

8. Lilian Knowles, Professor of Economic History,
   1921-6   65

9. Staff v. Students match at Malden, c. 1926   80

10. Interior of the Cobden Library   81

11. The Main Library   96

12. Roof of the new Houghton Street building, with
    Graham Wallas Room above   97

Notes on some of the Illustrations are given on pp. 127-8

I

A NEW START AFTER WAR

AT THE beginning of May 1919, while I was still Permanent Secretary to the Ministry of Food, I was invited by Sidney Webb to come to talk with him at the House of Lords, where he was sitting as a member of the Royal Commission on Coal Mines. His purpose in the talk proved to be that he wished to discover if I was prepared to give up the Civil Service and become Director of the School of Economics. The existing Director, Pember Reeves, was finishing at the end of May. In view of the need to obtain approval of the University Senate to any appointment of a Director, a June decision was imperative, though formal appointment could be dated from October 1st.

On June 6th, I wrote to Sidney from Edinburgh, where I had gone on Ministry of Food business to deal with a problem of potatoes, saying that I would accept appointment on the terms that he and I had discussed, and the appointment was duly made as from October 1st. This had what I hoped might prove an advantage to me, of enabling me to complete ten years of pensionable work as a Civil Servant and get something out of this to help me in old age,[1] as well as leaving the Ministry of Food tidy. It meant that for four months—June to September—the School had no Director.

Yet great developments affecting the School had been started already by Sidney Webb and others, and needed handling.

There was, first, a plan for establishing a Commerce Degree in the University of London, to be financed largely by an appeal to the City. The moving spirit of this was Sir Sydney Russell-Wells, a member of the University Senate who had

---

[1] As is recorded in *Power and Influence*, p. 160 and pp. 241-2, H.M. Treasury twice defeated this hope of mine.

become Vice-Chancellor in 1919 and remained Vice-Chancellor for three years.[1] Though himself a Lecturer in Clinical Medicine, he sat on the Senate not as a teacher, but as a repre-sentative of Convocation, elected by graduates. He represented thus the external side of the Senate and was clear that external students, those who sat for degrees by examination, however and wherever they studied, must get fair treatment. But he was thoroughly co-operative with the internal side and, in particular, with the School of Economics. He accepted con-centration at the School of all the formal teaching for the new Commerce Degree. He represented the readiness for co-opera-tion between all sides of the University, which came naturally for a number of years, when war had given place to hopes of peace.

There was, second, a large sum given by Sir Ernest Cassel and placed in the hands of trustees whose Chairman was Lord Haldane. From this came in February 1920 £150,000 as an endowment for Commerce Teaching, and grants for Modern Languages and Scholarships.

There was, third, a new building in prospect. The accom-modation at the School had been condemned as inadequate and seriously overcrowded, by an independent enquiry in 1913. Seven years later, in 1920, the School had the same building but half as many students again. Measures to remedy this had been taken before I came on the scene, by securing prospect of a site from the London County Council and £50,000 for building from the Commerce Degree Appeal.

This meant that from June to September Sidney Webb was in constant communication with me about the School of Economics which I was to direct. By the middle of July 1919 Sidney was urging me by all means to 'take hold' myself of the Commerce Degree Appeal that was being launched by the Vice-Chancellor of the University, Sir Sydney Russell-Wells. By the beginning of August he was putting to me the problem of the Librarian's salary, and the offer to the School of Richard Cobden's home at Dunford near Midhurst, as a place for reading parties, Summer Schools, and so forth.

[1] Born in 1869, after his Vice-Chancellorship he became in 1922 M.P. for the University of London till his death on July 14, 1924. He was succeeded as M.P. by Sir Ernest Graham Little. (See pp. 53-4 below.)

1   *Janet, having just received her O.B.E., with her four children*

2 *L.S.E. Rag, May 1920*

When Sidney Webb asked me in May 1919 to become Director of the London School of Economics, it was an institution with a brilliant past, and bright prospects for the future, largely through what he himself had done.

During the years of active war it had naturally lost students, but it was far from disappearing. In the three sessions 1915 to 1918 there were on average 1,242 students (600 men and 642 women) against 2,137 in 1912-3 (1,363 men and 774 women). And the School continued to issue its Calendar throughout the war, with as formidable a list as ever of teachers (practically all part-time), and of lecture courses. The Calendars from 1916 to 1918 were called Abridged Calendars, but were in fact larger than the full Calendars that preceded them, 112 against 108 pages; I have found no explanation yet of this early piece of London Economics.

Nor did the School at any time lack management. The Director, indeed, was increasingly absorbed in other tasks, becoming Chairman of a Bank, but the School was kept going by Miss Mactaggart, a Scot from Australia, as highly efficient Secretary and Dean, and a porter of stentorian voice called Dodson. The Library for a time was under the charge of McKillop, a cousin of Miss Mactaggart, also from Australia. But the Librarian of many years to come—B. M. Headicar— had been installed before Sidney approached me.

Ending of war showed at once the vitality of the School, with the number of students rising in the session 1918-9 above the pre-war level to 2,273, alike for men (1,415) and for women (858). The men included 224 American soldiers sent by the American Educational Mission in England.

Establishment of peace sent the total of students above the 3,000 mark for the first time, in the session 1919-20. There was an instant unparalleled demand for the service of the School in helping young people to a new life after war. Many young people, always having aimed at University courses, had been required to defer them for war service. Many others had decided during war service that they would try to go to a University for a degree before settling down to careers. The Government, recognizing the need, decided to award special scholarships and maintenance grants to secure University courses for war veterans, and a record flood of young people came pouring in to the Universities. 'Young people' in this connection, included women as well as men, for the School of Economics at least. The School in the first post-war session, 1919-20, had in its student body a larger proportion of women to men than in any peacetime session before or after.[1]

It was fortunate indeed that those interested in the School of Economics and its purposes had made so many plans in advance for money and a building site and new University courses. But, though all such things could be and were provided quickly by determined people, there was one thing at least whose provision was bound to take time.

When I started work officially as Director on October 1, 1919, though there were very few full-time teachers, there were a number of distinguished part-time teachers ready to go on. There was a surging mass of students—3,000 in my first session, as in my last session seventeen years later—but in 1919 there was practically nowhere to put either students or teachers. In my early years at the School some of our work had to be done in disused Army huts, waiting to be displaced by what is now Bush House. Space was the first problem that I met at the School, and forms the natural subject of the Chapter that follows this one.

Something had been done for building many years before, with the help of Passmore Edwards and the Prince Consort Act of 1843,[2] to make a Library; this was part of the Webb emphasis on research as more important even than teaching. But when I came to the School as Director to deal with 3,000 students, the Library had less than fifty readers' places. There were a few lecture rooms—never empty for airing. There were two tiny common rooms for students. Most harmful of all, there were hardly any rooms in which teachers could be alone or with selected students only. Professor Foxwell had to prepare his lectures in the Senior Common Room, and Theodore Gregory turned the Assistant Lecturers' Common Room into his study; at that time the junior staff were cut off from the Professors.

The most important decision of my early days was that any future buildings should be constructed on the principle of

[2] See p. 32 and Appendix I.
[1] See *The Epic of Clare Market*, pp. 30-31 and 46.

ensuring a private room for every regular teacher. Provision of this kind was not then, or for long afterwards, the rule in other London Colleges. So this was one of the rather numerous affairs in which the School of Economics came first into the field.

Vital as the need for more space was, on arrival as Director I found another problem as urgent and as important. We had to increase greatly the number of regular teachers and we had to bring teachers into touch with the administration of the School.

There were three full-time senior teachers when I reached the School—Professor Bowley for Statistics, Professor Sargent for Commerce, Dr. Lilian Knowles as Reader in Economic History. All these had been put up quite recently to what we regarded as a full salary.

There was a string of highly distinguished part-time teachers—Cannan, Foxwell, Lowes Dickinson, Pearce Higgins, Hobhouse, Mackinder, Mantoux, Seligman, Lees-Smith, Urwick, Wallas, Westermarck, Wolf. These, with the three full-timers, named above, with Sidney and myself and with two others—Lawrence Dicksee and W. T. Stephenson—whose position as between full-time and part-time was not altogether clear, made up a Professorial Council. But the Professorial Council met only twice in the year, and teachers appear to have had no other contact with the management of the School. One of the complaints made to me by a senior teacher, soon after my arrival, was that an assistant to him had been appointed without consultation or previous notice.

The School of Economics seemed to have got through as a one woman show in war. It was contrary to everything I believed to suppose that it should be a one man show in peace. One of my first acts as Director, in October 1919, was to ask the Professorial Council to appoint an Office Committee to advise me on administrative matters with an academic bearing, and this Committee did very useful work indeed. Three larger changes that followed at the earliest possible moment, in my second session, are described in a later chapter, on The Problem of Academic Self-Government.

In addition to the senior teaching staff and the distinguished part-timers, there were junior teachers, physically segregated.

They included Theodore Gregory, mentioned already as turning the Assistant Lecturers' Common Room into his study, and Hugh Dalton, both former students of the School. Gregory, being excluded on racial grounds from full war service that he wanted and offered, had been on the School staff from 1913 with intervals of teaching elsewhere. Dalton had begun studying at the School when he left Cambridge for London in 1910 to work for the Bar, won a Studentship at the School which led to his spending much of his time there and to finding a wife there in another student—Ruth Fox. After spending the War in war he returned to the School early in 1919 to work with Professor Cannan and became from 1922 to 1925 a Cassel Reader in Commerce. He resigned his University post as soon as he became a practising politician.

I liked both these young men at first sight and thereafter, and would have been happy to keep them always at the School. But they had too many other calls upon them. Hugh Dalton in his Memoirs says pleasant things about me as Director, and gives an amusing account of our varying relations, from the time when I was his boss academically to the time when, as Minister, he was my boss politically, getting me to produce super-perfect schemes for rationing coal or make new towns grow in County Durham.

In this exciting but laborious beginning at the School of Economics, I had one piece of great luck. I found myself able, within three months of starting at the School, to get absolutely first-rate assistance and to lay the foundations of a life-long partnership in work of every kind.

Jessy Mair, as she then was, Janet as she is called in this book hereafter, had agreed with her husband David when the first War ended that, with a view to providing for the education of their four children, she as well as he must earn. Various openings came her way—in the Factory Inspectors' department, in the Ministry of Health, in business—but for one reason or another none of these seemed to be just what she desired. She carried on through 1919 in the Ministry of Food, where she had many friends, dealing towards the end particularly with communal kitchens and canteens.

Meanwhile I was learning at first hand what I might need in the way of administrative help at the School. The formal

gap in the Directorship from June to September had made
little difference, because, even before June, Pember Reeves had
grown busy on other things and there was a natural manager
in charge: Miss Mactaggart. In an article on the School's
history which she wrote for the Students' Union long after,[1]
Janet, having told how Miss Mactaggart came to the School,
described her character and praised it highly:

'She had a fresh and forceful personality, vigorous in likes
and dislikes, and fearless in taking responsibility. Although
she had no University education, Miss Mactaggart's natural
ability made it possible for her to savour the atmosphere of a
college. Her robust determination to take part in every aspect
of its passing interests brought her into the very spirit of the
place.'

Of course I wanted and expected Miss Mactaggart to go on
with me. But she was older than I realised at first, having been
born in January 1861; she was in fact near to a normal retiring
age. It was clear that with the coming growth of the School
in building, teachers, students, subjects, more administration
would be needed. And it was clear to Miss Mactaggart that
she did not want to do everything. She described her presence
at the School as an accident; she had come first to earn enough
to buy an arm-chair and had stayed on. It became obvious that
what she would really like would be selection and advising of
students in the office of Dean, with someone else as business
secretary. Janet, with her combination of University training
and administrative experience, seemed to me made for such
a post, and she was welcomed by Miss Mactaggart. I asked her
to come and she did so—beginning work in December 1919.[2]

In June 1920 Miss Mactaggart fell ill suddenly and Janet
found herself at a moment's notice in charge of everything,
including getting out in three weeks the Calendar for 1920-1.[3]
The doctors held little hope of Miss Mactaggart recovering

---

[1] *Operation Dauntless* published in the *Clare Market Review* of
Michaelmas 1952. Not only this quotation but much of the substance of
what I wrote at the beginning of this chapter comes from Janet's article.

[2] A minute of mine dated December 18, 1919, speaks of putting a file
about the Red Lion public house into Mrs. Mair's folder.

[3] On the Calendar she got invaluable help from her husband David.
His work in the Civil Service Commission made the Calendars of nearly
all Universities familiar to him.

from her seizure enough to come back for many months, if at all. In fact retirement, coupled with kind treatment from the School, gave her a new lease of life. She was put on the Court of Governors and stayed there till the Session 1941-2; she died only in 1943. She had lived for some years with her sister in Italy and finally with relations in Australia.

In January 1921, by resolution of the Governors, Janet undertook the responsibility of both offices, that is to say of Dean and of Secretary, while continuing to be described as Secretary.

There was another very lucky thing for the School that happened about the time that I began there. This was the setting up of a University Grants Committee to allot to British Universities money provided by the Treasury. This Committee in their early days dealt directly and separately with each College in the University of London, and under their Chairman Sir William M'Cormick came in February 1920 to look at the School, and assess its needs and its chances of development. They came to so favourable a conclusion on its chances that, contrary to their habit at that time, in addition to increasing our annual grants they gave us a capital grant of £45,000 towards the buildings so desperately needed. Sir William M'Cormick had taught at St. Andrews, had taught Janet there, and thought very highly of her. I do not suggest that the School would not have received a capital grant without this happy accident, but certainly the chance of a grant was not lessened thereby; M'Cormick felt that money granted to the School would be well spent. I still think that it was spent well while Janet was concerned with it.

We were fortunate also in our personal relations with the London County Council where we dealt largely with Philippa Fawcett. She had been Senior Wrangler at Cambridge in the year after Janet's husband David had been Second Wrangler, which was also the year before Janet's brother William Philip became Third Wrangler. Personal contacts with the L.C.C. could not have been easier.

II

THE BATTLE OF HOUGHTON STREET

AS THE result of steps taken before my appointment by Sidney
Webb, Sydney Russell-Wells, Lord Haldane and others, aided
by the sympathetic attitude of the University Grants Committee, it proved possible to start a large new building scheme
at the School in my first year as Director. The foundation
stone was laid by the King on May 28, 1920. It was hoped, at
first, that the building might be ready for occupation in 1921,
but it was not completed and opened for two years, in May,
1922.

The starting of the new building by the King was made the
occasion by our students for a highly successful rag, pictured
opposite p. 17.

The value of the site for this extension, given by the London
County Council, was put at £50,000. The cost of building was
put at £140,000 provided as to £75,000 from the Commerce
Degree Fund raised by subscriptions of the business com-
munity in London, £45.000 from the Treasury, i.e. the
University Grants Committee, £15,000 from the London
County Council, and £5,000 from School reserves.

But this was a beginning only. The Director's Report for
1921-2,[1] from which the foregoing figures are taken, proceeds
at once to name another building extension, costing £25,000,
to take the place of sheds on land already owned by the
School in Clare Market.

And beyond this was the problem of Houghton Street
houses, destined to occupy the School authorities and many
other bodies for another five years. A start had been made on
one of these—the derelict Red Lion Public House. The School
had bought this before the end of 1919, and in January 1920,

[1]Read on Oration Day, June 24, 1922.

Janet, as Secretary. was asking the L.C.C. to licence its demolition. The licence came in February, but there was considerable delay in getting all the occupants out.

Meanwhile, attack was opened on the rest of Houghton Street—eight small houses and a corner building owned and used by St. Clement's Press—by letters to the L.C.C. valuer Frank Hunt, to the Chief Education Officer Sir Robert Blair, and to Sir William Berry of St. Clement's Press. All these letters, from 1920 to 1922, produced negative or dilatory results. And in 1923 no action at all seems to have been taken by the School about Houghton Street. The Director, Professors, and Governors alike were engaged with the problems raised by the visit in September 1923 of Beardsley Ruml of the Laura Spelman Rockefeller Memorial, the prospect of limitless dollars which it raised, and the issue of Social Biology (see Chapter VIII).

In 1924, a new attack on Houghton Street was launched by the School. Ought not the School to be authorized. in one way or another, to get a compulsory purchase order over Houghton Street, for a vital educational purpose? Charles Trevelyan, as President of the Board of Education, answered sympathetically in February; two of his officials, W. R. Barker (Legal Adviser) and Valentine Brown (Finance), pointed out that the London County Council regularly included in their General Powers Bill clauses allowing Borough Councils to make compulsory purchases for good cause. Why should not they do the same for the School of Economics in relation to Houghton Street?

It had taken the officials four months to make this suggestion. It took me four days to put it to Sir George Gater, Chief Education Officer of the L.C.C. In another four weeks the L.C.C. had sent a deputation to look at Houghton Street and had agreed to include what we wanted in their General Powers Bill—provided that it did not cost them anything.

This wasn't easy to promise in July 1924. By the devoted help of one of our Commerce Degree Governors, J. Wilson Potter, we had persuaded the London Senate to hand over to us for buying houses, £7,000 of Commerce Degree money for which there was no other use.[1] But £7,000 was not nearly enough.

So I dashed off to America, on the plea of attending the British Association at Toronto, but really to see my friends of the Laura Spelman Rockefeller Memorial. I came back in October with sufficient prospect of dollars to justify us in asking the London Senate to support our plea to the L.C.C. to put the compulsory purchase of Houghton Street into their General Powers Bill now being drafted.

Without a Senate resolution, the L.C.C. would have done nothing for us. But the Senate played up nobly. They were still in the halcyon days of post-war co-operation, before, as Vice-Chancellor, I had to get the Bloomsbury Site through and Rockefeller millions accepted by five votes, or sometimes three votes. In October 1924 the Senate were 'of opinion that it is of the utmost importance that the property in Houghton Street therein referred to should be acquired for the purposes of the London School of Economics'.

Of course, this did not end the battle. We had still to fight our clause through the House of Commons Private Bills Committee against opposition by the *Financial Times* as owners of St. Clement's Press, by Sporting Publications, by a grocer, a hairdresser and other would-be dwellers in Houghton Street. I spent most of April 2, 1925, answering questions by counsel for us or against us. 'We had ludicrously too little accommodation; with two important teachers in each room giving individual teaching simultaneously to different pupils, with lectures running continuously in the same room without change of air.' The question came, of course, why we didn't move somewhere else, and I answered: 'It is obviously possible, though difficult, to send printing elsewhere. It is not possible to send our lecturers or students elsewhere.'

In the end, by giving up one of the eight houses that we had asked for, we won all the rest. On August 7, 1925, the General Powers Bill of the L.C.C. with our Clause 6 in it received the Royal Assent. We had made a typical British compromise.

[1] In reporting Wilson Potter's good deed to Steel-Maitland our Chairman of Governors, I observed that 'I find it quite impossible to get into debt, but hope that Houghton Street may accomplish this'.

Of course, we had to wait for the houses. A year later, in 1926, we were still begging the Senate to ask the L.C.C. to exercise the compulsory powers it now possessed. And the Senate persuaded the L.C.C. to give us vacant possession by June 30, 1927, seven and a half years after Janet had made her first request to Frank Hunt for help from the L.C.C. on Houghton Street.

How fortunate for Colleges and Public Authorities that they live for ever! How sad for the young that they may sometimes miss the chance of University life in just the three years when it is needed!

I have told the story of Houghton Street at some length, because it is on the whole encouraging. It shows that people with a good cause can get it through if they know the arts of persuasion and will take whatever trouble is needed.

But they must have the arts of persuasion. The School turned from defeat towards victory when it convinced the experts of the Board of Education of our need and persuaded them to meet our need. In this, as it happened, Janet, as the new Secretary of the School, played an important part.

I have told the story also because its end is so pleasant. The St. Clement's Press had fought us to the last moment. They took their defeat like gentlemen. They were left with a corner building which they valued at £14,000, which we wanted for the School, but for which we felt unable to pay more than £11,000. Sir William Berry cut the knot by giving us £1,500 as a gift from himself and £1,500 from his brother, to turn £11,000 into £14,000.

But even that was not the end. There is a happy sequel today, in 1959. The St. Clement's Press, which fought us so hard on Houghton Street and acted so generously in defeat, is at the moment dismantling its main building also, on the north of Clare Market. The School will spread there. This whole central spot in London will serve a unique purpose, in education for a better world. If only London as a whole could be planned as rationally, how marvellous it would be.

Nor, of course, was our first victory in Houghton Street the end of our spreading and building there. The first seven Houghton Street houses, obtained by compulsion in 1925, reached our hands at last in 1927. Year after year thereafter, my Annual Report on the School recorded a fresh extension. In 1927 we signed a building contract, not only for Houghton Street, but for two new floors, including the Founders' Room, on our main building. In 1928, I reckoned that we had added in one year 18,000 square feet to our space, making 78,000 square feet altogether, as compared with 14,000 feet in total that we had occupied eight years before. In 1929 came more buying by agreement in Houghton Street: the Holborn Estate School and two houses. In 1931, with the support of the new University Court, we gave Houghton Street another dose of compulsory acquisition through the L.C.C. We were successful again, though, not long after, such procedure was brought to an end.

The space that we were seeking to add to our use was always anything but lecture space. At the request of the Rockefeller Foundation, the School prepared for them once a Review of the Activities and Development of the School between 1923 and 1937. The Review gives interesting figures on our physical growth in that period.

Between 1923 and 1937, our total space for all purposes grew in round figures from 51,000 to 134,000 square feet, just over two and a half times. Our social and administrative rooms grew nearly in the same proportion, though a little less, say two and one third times. The greatest increases were in Library and Seminar rooms—more than five times; in Teachers' Rooms—well over four times; in Circulation (inevitable as the building spread) a little over three times. The Lecture Rooms practically did not grow at all. While other accommodation had risen anything from two and a half to five times, the Lecture Rooms were larger only by one sixth.[1]

For my first twelve years we seemed always to be building somewhere. We had to do this because our space was filled to capacity from nine in the morning to nine at night, with more and more students coming to us regularly by day for all their waking time, with our evening work as large as ever. And we stuck to our first decision that University life requires personal contact between the teacher and the pupil; so the seminar

[1] Readers will I hope find it of interest to compare the figures of past accommodation with the accommodation today (1959) as given in the Appendix of Statistics.

rooms and the teachers' rooms led the way in growth.

Janet and I were crossword fans, familiar with the Oxford Dictionary of Quotations, and Wordsworth fans also. We adapted to our needs Christopher North's view of 1829 about His Majesty's dominions: The School of Economics was that part of the University of London on which the concrete never sets. We adapted optimistically to our growing School Wordsworth's lines on the lovely child amid dancing rivulets:

> And beauty born of hammering sound
> Shall pass into her face.

Wordsworth had written 'murmuring' in place of hammering. Whether our building workmen murmured or not, I never learned. They hammered certainly, while professors lectured.

Every now and again it crossed our minds, particularly after the Bloomsbury site was won, to ask whether it might have been wiser, in place of fighting for Houghton Street, to move ourselves to the new University centre. By then it was already too late to consider such a move. Apart from that, I am certain now that the decision on placing which Sidney Webb had taken when he got Passmore Edwards Hall built and which we followed faithfully was right. The School of Economics and Political Science as a unique place of resort for teachers, researchers and students in Britain, had to be just where it was, equally accessible to those who needed it, wherever they lived in London or near it. When the battle for Houghton Street was on, our argument to this effect had convinced in turn the University Senate, the Board of Education, the London County Council, and the House of Commons Committee on Private Bills.

Equal accessibility for all was and is the decisive reason on merits for keeping the School of Economics where it was and is—in Clare Market. But Clare Market is not making history for the first time today.

From James I to Queen Anne, it was the abode of residential aristocracy, sometimes serious, sometimes flippant, like the bloods and bucks of the Restoration. And Lords of those days, like Lords today, sometimes wanted more money. So Lord Clare found land for a butchers' market and the judgment of these butchers became the standard of failure or success in the theatres and taverns that shared the region with them. 'According to the butchers of Clare Market' was the operative phrase.

There followed a degeneration immortalized by Dickens in *Bleak House*, with Jo sweeping his crossing, with houses full of rats and of criminals of every kind—a 'doomed quarter', a slum marked out for clearance. But then came Sidney. And then—

'The fame of Clare Market in its seventeenth century grandeur, and its decline for 150 years into one of the most squalid resorts of notorious criminals and of the homeless destitute, is forgotten now. Who knows but that its final apotheosis may be in its reputation as the site of a unique University institution of international reputation and eminence recognized as such the world over. And all *that* in just sixty years!'

So Janet wrote for the Clare Market Review in *Sixty Years On*.[1]

[1] Published in Summer Term 1956.

III

STUDENTS AND
THEIR PROBLEMS

THE STUDENTS CHANGE

DURING my time as Director, the student body at the School of Economics remained almost the same in total number. In 1919-20 we had 3,016 students altogether and in 1936-7 we had 3,000. In between, apart from three years of temporary decline between 1921 and 1924, chiefly in women students, our total fluctuated only from about 2,800 to 3,000. But, while the total number of students remained much the same throughout my Directorate, the character of the student body changed completely and this changed as completely the work of the School.

The change in the character of the student body can be put in two sentences. At the beginning of my time, one third of all our students, roughly 1,000 out of 3,000, were taking full courses for a degree, diploma, certificate, or something like it, and two thirds, 2,000 out of 3,000, were occasional students, paying fees for one or more lectures which they wished specially to attend or to which their employers sent them. At the end of my time, two thirds of all our students, 2,000 out of 3,000, were taking full courses and one third, 1,000 out of 3,000, were occasionals. The proportions of full course and occasional study in the School had been reversed.

The full-course students fell under two heads. Those registered at the School itself and paying their fees to it were described as its regular students, even though they might receive some of their teaching in another college by arrangement with the School, which met the cost from its fees. There were other students registered for a full course at

30

some other college, but coming to the School for part of their teaching; by the School they were described as inter-collegiate students.

The doubling of full-course students, whether called regular or called inter-collegiate, and the halving of the occasionals, meant that *on an average* of the 3,000, each student made more demands on its services of teaching, library, refectory, common room, athletics, and more and more accommodation had to be provided to meet the demand, throughout my Directorate.

The substitution of 2,000 full-course and 1,000 occasional students by 1937, for the 1,000 full-course and 2,000 occasional students of 1919-20 is the major general change in the student body during my Directorate. But there are special developments also of much interest, and there are some things of interest which did not change.

One development was the growth of inter-collegiate arrangements, making it possible for a student to get the teaching he needed just where he could get it best. In my Directorate, inter-collegiate arrangements, though by no means confined to law teaching, developed most rapidly in that subject, by co-operation between University College, King's College and the School. The inter-collegiate students of the School, that is those coming to it from other colleges, having numbered 140 in my first year, were 597 in my last year; they had multiplied more than four times.

Another marked rise was in the number of students coming to the School from overseas. In 1919-20 we had 291 and in 1936-7 we had 717, an increase of two and a half times. Towards the end of this time they were coming from fifty different countries. The international appeal of the School has always been one of its strongest points.

Yet a third rise related to higher degrees. As might be expected, work for such degrees increased greatly as the School grew in strength and reputation. From 1919-20 to 1936-7 first degree students little more than doubled, rising from 376 to 827, while the rise from 1920-21 was even less— little more than fifty per cent. Higher degree students, from being thirty-two in 1919-20 and forty-seven in 1920-1, increased to 293 and 1936-7, rises of about nine and about six times respectively.

From these cheering changes in the student body, it is interesting to turn to one or two things which did not change materially in my Directorate.

One was the proportion between the sexes. Apart from a few special years, like 1919-20 and 1923-7,[1] this proportion is much the same throughout my period—one woman to three men. That holds only if all students, whether regular or occasional, or day or evening students, are taken together. If we look at evening students only, men usually outnumber women six to eight times; by contrast the proportion of women is much greater by day.

Another thing that did not change in my Directorate was the division of our regular students as between day and evening study. To make this point clear, I must explain that the term full-course study, as I have used it above, does not mean full-time study. The School had been started largely for evening work. It was and is possible for a person working for his living by day to take at the School a full course for a degree as an evening student, and the teaching of the School was designed for this.

In preparing this account of my time as Director, I was much interested to find that, from its beginning in 1919 to its end in 1937, the division of regular students as between day and evening study remained the same. Taking the first three years 1920 to 1923 together (to avoid risk of error through something exceptional in one year) sixty-two per cent of the regular students came by day and thirty-eight per cent in the evening. Taking the last three years 1934-7 together, the percentage of day students is sixty-one and that of evening students is thirty-nine; the division between day and evening study is as nearly as possible the same. This is a most interesting result for two reasons. First, it shows how right Sidney Webb had been, when as Chairman of the Technical Education Board in 1893, he had made it a condition of giving money to the School or any other teaching

[1] These and other special years are considered in the Appendix of Statistics.

3 *Old Houghton Street houses*

4 *The Army Class, 1930-31, outside the old front door*

institution, that the institution should provide for evening study. Second, it means that the School buildings, from 1919 to 1937, were occupied more fully than any other place of study probably than can be found anywhere in the world.[1]

THE NEEDS OF STUDENTS

The outstanding features of Janet's and my time at the School on the student side were the substitution of regular for occasional work there, its growing co-operation with other colleges in London, and its growing attraction to students from all over the world. Though we could not, when we arrived there, guess the scale of the coming change, we could sense it coming. What should we do about it?

Janet and I had both been intensely happy as University students, she at St. Andrews, I at Balliol. We set ourselves, from the beginning of our time at Houghton Street, to re-create the conditions of this student happiness there. Adapting some words which I used in one of my later Annual Reports on the School, we set ourselves to prove that a full University life did not depend upon living together in a medieval building. These words, of course, were put into my mouth by Janet; she had discovered it in her time at St. Andrews. It was easy for me to accept her words; very few of the buildings at Balliol were medieval, yet my life there from 1897 to 1902 was as full as any young man could desire—unless he wanted young women also.

We both knew that a full University life for a student depended on personal contacts of two kinds: with an individual teacher and with other students. Could we bring about such personal contacts for a body of students so much larger than that of Balliol or St. Andrews?

Encouragement of contact between one student and another was simple and action came quickly. From its earliest days there had been a very active Students Union in the School, organizing meetings, discussions, and societies of many kinds, and launching in the *Clare Market Review* a quarterly

[1] As is shown in the Notes on Table A in the Appendix of Statistics though there is still a substantial number of evening students taking full courses, the proportion to day students is smaller in 1959 than it was in 1937.

periodical which has continued from that day to this. But the Union was not all embracing. Membership of it depended on a student deciding to join it and pay the subscription.

As from the beginning of the session 1920-1, the Students Union was re-organized. All regular students, that is all those paying the composition fee for a degree course or other course of full study, became automatically full members of the Union. Others became limited members only, but could obtain full privileges by additional voluntary subscriptions. The fees charged by the School included the Union subscription, which was paid over to the Union by the School.

On the financial re-organization there followed, as part of our building programme and as rapidly as possible, the material facilities for life together in the School—a theatre for full debates, a refectory large enough for the student numbers, common rooms and rooms for society meetings. What contact between one student and another came to be before we ended at L.S.E. and how full it was is shown later in this chapter.

Securing of adequate contacts between students and teachers was not so simple and took longer. It meant, of course, finding and paying more teachers; this is dealt with in my next chapter. It meant providing a separate room for every regular teacher at least, so that he could deal personally and alone with students assigned to him; this was accepted as one of the vital aims in our building plans; but building took time even in the 1920's. It meant attaching every regular student, throughout his course, to one teacher or another. Here we encountered a difficulty, from the nature of the study courses for the degrees with which the school was chiefly concerned. Broadly they involved a general course common to all students for one year in preparing for an 'intermediate' examination, followed by specialization for two years in an Honours subject. In these later years each student was assigned automatically to a particular teacher and made personal contact with that teacher. In his first year a student had no such automatic contact; no teacher need be interested in him.

To remedy this, we introduced as soon as we could a system of Advisers of Studies for first year students, attaching them in groups of eight to twelve to a teacher for whom they wrote essays on general subjects, and I offered a Director's Prize for competition among the essayists.

This plan involved naturally a good deal of discussion with the teachers and could not be put into action before my fourth session—1923-4. In proposing the plan, I fear that I was influenced by my Balliol experience, with the stimulating effect on me of its first year essays unrelated to anything that I was studying. In introducing first year essays at the School of Economics I made the concession that the subjects, though general, should be connected with economics and political science. The real point of the proceeding lay in giving to every regular student, from the beginning, a friend in the teaching staff—the nearest approach that, with our numbers and our conditions, we could make to the Oxford tutorial system as I knew it.

Re-organizing the Students Union and establishing First Year Advisers did not meet all the needs of our new Student Body, in making it feel at home and at one. We had to provide also for physical exercise in athletics, for something that would emphasise the School as a community, and possibly for something that might give occasions for meeting away from Houghton Street. Action to meet the first of the three requirements—for athletic facilities—came at once; in this book it falls to a later chapter on 'Economists at Play'. Action to meet the second requirement came soon, by the establishing in 1922 of a Commemoration Week. Something to meet the third need was done at once, but did not last. I suspect that most students today are meeting this need for themselves.

Commemoration Week, held at the end of the term in June, combined light and serious activities, ranging from cricket and tennis matches at Malden (so far as possible between staff and students), a play by students, and a dance, to an Oration Day on which an Annual Report by me on the work of the School was followed by an Address from a distinguished visitor. There was at first also a School Dinner in Commemoration Week, but in 1930 it was decided that the end of Michaelmas Term was better than June for dinners, and the dance was given pride of place as the last affair of all, a day after the Oration was well over, and without competition; I suspect that this change reflected the greater average youth of our students; most of us have been young enough once to prefer dancing with other young people to dining with Professors.

I made my Report into a means of saying farewell to students leaving, and with Janet I took to inviting the Executive of the Students Union to a dinner or small reception, also as a rule in winter, to meet teachers or special governors. I have just heard, while writing this book, of a pleasant episode at the first of these dinners, in 1920, that was attended by Sidney and Beatrice. The President of the Union of that time (for many years now a Professor at the School) found himself seated between the star guests and talking to Sidney about his personal difficulty in doing research—he didn't seem to have a good enough brain. Sidney answered: 'excellent research is done by people of quite ordinary brain, like myself; go on!' Typical Sidney kindness!

The first Commemoration Week was held in 1922 and the first orator was H. H. Asquith. The second orator in 1923 was to have been a Conservative—Lord Chancellor Cave, to keep the political balance true, but he fell ill at the last moment. Being on friendly terms with Winston Churchill, then in the wilderness, I tried to persuade him to take Lord Cave's place. I failed in that, but he promised to come next year, did come and made on June 27th a superb oration urging students to become masters of writing English. In the course of it he attacked compulsory Latin in Universities with the utmost vigour. To enforce classical study as a main foundation of study was 'an absurd mistake'. It had been even more absurd with the new pronunciation of Latin. He in his youth had learned and liked to say *audire*. Now he was told to say 'ow-dearie'. This brought down the house.

The Commemoration meeting which should have been addressed by Lord Cave in June 1923, was replaced by an even grander affair—a Mansion House Luncheon to celebrate the first three years of the Commerce Degree. Among many other notabilities of every kind, it was attended by the President of the Board of Education, then Mr. E. F. L. Wood, now Lord Halifax. He made a very pleasant principal speech.

Lord Cave gave his Oration in due course, recommending economics as a compulsory study for public men. I observed to a neighbour that it would at least be better for them than compulsory Latin.

The most popular and successful of our Oration Days came in 1928, when the Annual Report, instead of being read by me, was 'submitted in silence' and there was no Oration at all. The Prince of Wales, as he was then, came as our principal guest. After dinner, Jelly d'Aranyi played to him and the rest of us; he made a delightful nonsensical speech as having been for six years the only M.Comm. in the world; wound up with 'Let us get on with the Dance'; and was as good as his conclusion — dancing with our students like anything. My mother, who was deaf, came away from the party with a note in the Prince's own hand expressing his pleasure in being there.

In addition to contributing my Annual Report to Commemoration Week, I did one other thing personally to emphasise the purpose and community of the School. I gave an Address to New Students at the beginning of each session in nearly every year from 1921 to 1936.

Janet found a more excellent way of bringing people together in the School, by music rather than words. She organized Lunch Hour Concerts from November 1925 onwards and they attracted good audiences. At one time, early in 1928, the concerts had to be abandoned because they could not compete for hearing with the building that had begun once more. But when building came to an end the concerts began again and they continue to this day. Janet encouraged music also in another way by giving a Jessy Mair Cup for music, which is awarded still each year to a student.

Janet and I together were active in getting an L.S.E. Literary Society launched, and found a delightfully encouraging reception both among the students and among distinguished guests, like Walter de la Mare, Harold Monro, Dr. Caroline Spurgeon and S. A. Williams of the *London Mercury*, whom we lured to talk to us. I could not refuse to be the first President, and gave an opening address on Youth and Age in Literature which, after I had contrasted the phenomenon of youthful eighteenth century poets and Jane Austen in England with the agedness of Greek dramatists, led to vigorous discussion not precisely on my subject. 'The

possible connection between periods of national greatness and
outbursts of literary energy was suggested but fairly conclu-
sively denied by Sir William Beveridge.' So this affair was
recorded by a student who now holds an important place in
the organization of the National Health Service.

But the Literary Society was as far as possible from just
listening to the old. It produced its own papers, and it formed
an excellent habit of reading poetry out loud to itself, working
through the centuries from before 1616 to 1900 with a
divagation to Modern American Poets. And annually the
Society was young enough to ramble over the Cotswolds in
July, leading to supper at Kensington with 'Mrs. Mair'.

There was a Commerce Society also at the School, which I
am said to have addressed on the advantages of social life at
the older universities, making a plea for development of social
life at least as much in our new School. Given that, an internal
London student would become a better educated person than
one who had been to an ancient university.

In the upshot, of course (apart from some of the student
problems noted in my next section) the social life of the
students owed more to the students themselves, as organized
in the Students Union, than to any older friend. I cannot
illustrate this better than by two extracts from one of my
Annual Reports on the School delivered in the slightly
troubled year 1934.

'For the Students Union, the session has been one of novel
and exciting experiences, including three presidential elections
in six months, the debating of several votes of censure on the
Executive Committee and constitutional controversies, both
as to the Union itself and to its relations to the School authorities. Through all these disturbances, the social life of the
School, in clubs and societies, has continued with unabated
vigour.'

In the course of discussions with the Union I asked for a
return showing what social and athletic activities had actually
occupied different parts of our building during the session
1933-4. The result was prodigious.

'This return shows that during twenty-six weeks of the
session fifty different clubs and societies have held between
them nearly a thousand meetings a week, or seven meetings

on each of the five weekdays on which the School is in action. The fifty clubs and societies include twenty for different forms of athletics from Rugby football to folk-dancing, nineteen centring on some special interest from banking to music or religion, from India to the drama or the assistance of German refugees; seven (including University as well as School societies) of a political character, and four which appear to be purely social for particular groups of students.

'These student societies have been accommodated in some twenty-five different rooms of the building, being fitted, in accordance with their size, into the rooms available at their time of meeting. The return excludes many meetings of Committees, such as those held in the offices set aside for the Union, as well as meetings of staff societies and of the Old Students' Association.'

*

In my University days sixty years ago, as in those of Arthur Hugh Clough born sixty years before me, it had been common for Balliol men to devote part of their vacations to reading parties, with or without a don to guide them; I remember to this day how much I gained thereby. When it seemed possible, on my arrival at the School, that it would possess a house of its own where reading parties could be held and social life of many kinds organized, I jumped at the chance.

Dunford House, near Midhurst, formerly the residence of Richard Cobden, was offered to the School by his daughter Mrs. Cobden Unwin in 1919 and was presented formally in December 1921, as a country house for rest study and research and for educational and other conferences. In my first years at the School I devoted much energy to Dunford House, organizing meetings there, taking important people like Sir William M'Cormick there, and so on. But the use of the house did not work out as the donors expected. After three years of trial it was re-purchased by them in July 1923, and the money paid for it was used to establish the Cobden Library of International Trade as part of the Library equipment of the School.

In view of the prospective loss of Dunford House, I wrote to Sidney Webb in February 1924, sending him a prospectus

THE SCHOOL OF ECONOMICS

of my parents' house at Pitfold, Hindhead, with the suggestion
that if the Governors wanted, I and my mother would lend
t to the School for three years with no commitment of the
School beyond; 'the terms, of course, would have to be such
that I could not possibly do anything but make a loss out of
it, and should pay for improvements'.

There was this amount of appropriateness in my offer—that
Sidney's fellow Fabian Bernard Shaw had spent his honeymoon in Pitfold and that somewhat later my gentle-hearted
father had burnt *Candida* under a copper-beech on the lawn
there, as a shocking book. So Pitfold, like the School, illustrated both Fabianism and differences of opinion.[1]

I did not expect anything to come of my suggestion to
Sidney about Pitfold. Nor did it.

A little later, Janet acquired a bungalow called Green
Street, near Avebury in Wiltshire, which became the recurrent
resort of many teachers of the School from Graham Wallas
downwards and many students.

It entertained distinguished visitors from abroad like André
Siegfried and Wesley Mitchell. Once even it entertained
Sidney and Beatrice. And walking parties were organized
from it. Green Street, to which one could go only by invitation
of its owner, was not, of course, in any sense an alternative to
Dunford House. But it has seemed worth while to give the
names of some of its visitors and a few photographs to
illustrate the kind of life that Janet tried to live and make for
others from the School.[2]

STUDENTS HAVE THEIR PROBLEMS

The students naturally regarded themselves as the main
purpose of the School, if not the only purpose. In order to get
the most they could from the School they had to solve a
number of problems. There was for some, at the outset, the
problem of getting into the School. There was for many or
most, at the other end of their time, the problem of finding
suitable employment. There was for many need for help and
kindness from senior members of the School not connected

[1] Pitfold is now in full use as staff-quarters of a flourishing secondary
grammar school with 400 to 500 boys and girls from the neighbourhood
in attendance. The copper-beech tree is as beautiful as ever.
[2] See between pp. 48 and 49, and on p. 128.

with their studies. There was every now and again a problem of rules and discipline.

During the period under review, the School never limited the number of students it would admit if they appeared to be qualified. Every now and again the Director was forced to contemplate the possible need for numerical limit if students continued to present themselves in excess of the room available. But it always proved just possible to avoid this by enlarging the School building. We did not like to reject qualified students, because there was no alternative to the School, in its main range of teaching, in London.

Admission to the School, however, involved payment of a fee. The School, like other Colleges, offered Entrance Scholarships, with a view to attracting able students to come, even if they could not afford the fee. Janet and I liked, whenever we could, to keep in touch with the election of scholars, by way of understanding the detailed work of the School. I give below a conversation which I had with my mother one year, when she was living with me, to show the pleasant character of this scholarship affair.

'We were electing to entrance scholarships at the School on Tuesday and were able to elect the School's first grandchild, i.e. a daughter of a former student. We're so young that the generations have only just begun to return to us.

'The election was a very pleasant proceeding. We interviewed them one by one; then, having four scholarships and being unable to choose between the best five candidates, we had them all in together and told them that as we couldn't decide we'd give each of them a scholarship. The cheerful grin that rose up in all five faces as they realized that they had been successful was very pleasant!

'Then I had the sad task of breaking the news to the unsuccessful. One poor boy literally cried!

'He was the son of an East End Jew—his father sells second-hand boxes at Stepney. If he got nothing he would have to go out to work at once. He felt the shades of the prison house closing on him! He was quite a nice boy, and we'll probably give him a bursary which will enable him to get a State Scholarship as well.

'It was a cheering interview for two reasons.

(1) The candidates were definitely better than last year.
(2) Nearly all, when I asked them what they meant to do in
life, said they weren't sure. They were coming to us to get a
University education and then see what they could do, not
simply to get a degree or training for a particular vocation.

'One bright lad, being asked what books on economics he
had read, said *Public Finance*, a book written by Dr. Dalton
who was questioning him. It was just like the middy who was
asked to name three admirals. You remember the *Punch*
story. He said, 'Nelson, Blake—and I didn't quite catch your
name, Sir.' (He was being examined by an Admiral.)

'The School is really a delightful place and absurdly
successful just now.'

*

At the other end of their course most students meet another
problem; that of finding employment of the kind that they
desire most.

The School, particularly after the institution of the Commerce Degree, attached special importance to the question of
appointments for students, established close co-operation with
the University Commerce Degree Bureau, and from the
Calendar for 1925-6 onwards published regularly lists of
appointments gained. By 1929 I felt able to report that the
placing of students in business was becoming easier each year.
In the slump of 1932-4 placing may well have become harder
again, but our answer was to establish a full-time Appointments Officer at the School, with excellent results. In my
Report given in June 1935 I announced a list of appointments
much longer than ever before, with 200 names in it. I attri-
buted this to three factors—to better demand as the depression
passed, to having our own Appointments Officer, and to his
keeping close contact with our graduates.

Students are not students only. They are young human
beings often away from their parents and needing the help
that parents give. They might get such help from a sympathetic teacher, not too busy with teaching. Many of our
students between 1919 and 1937, received it in fact from the
Secretary to the School, my Janet. If I had not known this
before, I should know it now from the many letters that I

have received after her death, from people who knew her at the School.

The letters abound with references, not merely to Janet's 'vital personality' or devoted work or tremendous beneficial influence, but to her kindness and courtesy and helpfulness to everyone with whom she had to deal. It is sufficient for me to give here half a dozen such tributes only. I print one tribute later, in the place that is most appropriate for it.

'We shall always remember her kindness to undergraduates. We both owe her a debt of gratitude for her friendliness and humour, particularly in the Literary Society and at the time of our marriage.'

'Lady Beveridge was very kind to me as an impoverished L.S.E. student of 1933 and I have always been grateful to her.'

'For me she was always part of my post-graduate student days.'

'For me Janet was a part of my undergraduate years and an essential and vital element in my pleasant memories of those wonderful times at L.S.E. with the friendly hospitable weekends at Avebury.'

'I shall always be grateful for her kindness to me and for all the help she gave me in deciding my future.'

'She played such a large part in my early life in this country and showed me so much kindness that for this reason alone her memory will always be dear to me. But she was an unforgettable personality for all who had the good luck to meet her. She will live forever in the annals of the School.'

*

University students not only have problems of their own but at times present problems to the elders in charge of them problems of discipline. They are in process of change from being children governed by others to being adults who should have learned to govern themselves. So far as I know in Janet's and my time at the School we had only two cases of discipline that called for attention—both in the same year, 1934.

In one case, six or seven students, led by a very red politician from America, having produced or acquired a pamphlet called the *Student Vanguard,* insisted on selling it in the School even after they had been forbidden to do so. I suspended them, keeping them out of the School, and reported to the Emergency Committee, which, after seeing the students, expelled two (one subject to forgiveness by me later) and accepted apologies from the rest. What was much more important, with my full consent they recommended, and the Governors in due course agreed, that the Director's powers in respect of expulsion, suspension and so forth, should be formally limited to interim action pending decision by the Emergency Committee. This was entirely in accord with my policy, described elsewhere,[1] of persuading Governors and teachers to feel responsibility for the School. It is a curious fact that the American leader of the revolt, whom the Emergency Committee after full consideration felt to be better suited to the United States than to the School, had been not only President of our Students Union, but also a paid research assistant to one of our teachers.

In the other case, occurring soon after, a number of students went on strike against the School Refectory and made a demonstration of going outside for food. The manager of the Refectory after many years of good service was in failing health just then. We pensioned her off and replaced her. So far as I know, there was no other strike in my time. But, as we all know, Refectories are there to be shot at.

In ending my Annual Report on the School in the session 1933-4, which I gave on June 21, 1934, I made an oddly solemn reference to these troubles, as a paradox:

'When the history of our School comes to be written it will have to be recorded that this session of unexampled physical peace in the School has been a session of acute psychological disturbance. The future historian may be able to explain this paradox himself or he may call in aid his colleagues from a neighbouring field—economics, psychology, politics, or some other study.'

As today I am writing, not indeed the history of the School, but my story as a contribution to history, I feel rash enough to offer an explanation of our psychological disturbance of 1934 on my own, without calling on others for aid. It was due to a combination of the youth of the School with my old friend— the Trade Cycle. 1933 and 1934 were years of unparalleled

[1] Chapter VII.

44

unemployment, of unhappiness, and of resentment of unhappiness throughout the industrial world. It affected the life of the School in relation not only to students but also, as I shall record in my next chapter, in relation to teachers, and raised a problem there for everyone interested in the School.

Having said so much about psychological disturbances in the School, I feel bound to add a corrective from a letter which came to me after Janet's death from a student who was there in that time and is now in an excellent business position:

'Those who were undergraduates of L.S.E. during your Directorship will have had happy memories of the constant interest Lady Beveridge took in their welfare. The early 1930's, when graduate unemployment was relatively high, could have been a breeding ground for discontent of all kinds in the L.S.E. That, on the contrary, a warm and friendly atmosphere prevailed was a measure of your and Lady Beveridge's success in preserving the humanities.'

IV

TEACHERS AND THEIR
PROBLEMS

TEACHERS MUST LIVE

THE School of Economics was the first college in London to establish £1,000 a year as minimum salary for full-time Professors. The School did this for two Professors, A. L. Bowley and A. J. Sargent in 1919 even before I became Director formally, though with my full consent and I think to some extent at my urging. Sidney and Beatrice said often how much their own work of research had depended on freedom from financial worries. And they wanted professors not only to teach but to research.

Janet and I thought that Professors should be free from financial worries, even though they had children. We were convinced supporters of Eleanor Rathbone. At the earliest moment when we could manage it, in 1925, we persuaded the Governors to make the School the first college anywhere in Britain to add educational allowances to the salaries of teachers and senior administrators. When it was introduced in 1925, the allowance was £30 a year for each child between thirteen and twenty-three while in full-time attendance at a place of approved education. Some of the teachers of the School felt doubtful about educational allowances,[1] but with the support of Sir Josiah Stamp, who had become Vice-Chairman of the Governors, we got our proposal through.

These first educational allowances were on a modest scale but in 1927-8 the School made a general improvement of teachers' remuneration, with a new salary scale for full-time Professors, and with educational allowances of £30 a year from birth to the age of thirteen, followed by £60 a year to

[1] See p. 49 below for Lilian Knowles' view.

46

the age of twenty-three for children in full-time attendance at a place of approved education. These allowances applied to the administrative staff as well as to all teachers.

In another five years, the Governors had come to realize that the regular workers in the School included not teachers and administrators only, but porters, refectory staff and others on whose service the comfort of everyone depended. They established for such persons both a Group Pensions Scheme and educational allowances for children between fourteen and nineteen in regular attendance at a post-primary educational institution of recognized standing.

The School recognized that all who served it in whatever capacity deserved consideration. The porter staff in particular produced a number of outstanding figures, from Dobson who, when he left in 1924, had been adviser in general for 20 years, through Walter Wilson, who succeeded him as head-porter, with 51 years of total service from 1906 to 1957, and Joseph Hurd—a star performer in the Mock Trials, to George Panormo still in School service today after 47 years. George was one of the School representatives at the Memorial Service to Janet in May 1959.

The scales of salary at the School had been the subject of review, in comparison with those of other University institutions, four years before, but a Committee of Governors in 1928-9 made a further examination leading to the following main conclusions:

'The scales of pensionable salary taken as a whole are certainly better than those in any comparable London College and will probably stand comparison with those of most British Universities. Having regard, however, to the unique position of the School in the field of the social sciences, it is in the view of the Committee essential that the professorial salaries shall be such as, taking into account all other factors, can be relied on to attract to the School teachers of outstanding eminence in their subjects.'

The practical inference from this was to make the normal professorial salary no longer £1,000 a year but £1,000 rising to £1,250 after five years, while not excluding more for good reason; the School at that moment had two Professors at £1,500 a year.

Having made improvements of normal scale for Professors and others, the Governors laid down a new provision about outside work: that the permission of the School should be required for any outside paid work by full-time teachers, other than examining for the School or a University and occasional writing and the giving of one or two special lectures. This was the provision applied six years later to an arrangement made by Professor Laski to write regular articles for the *Daily Herald*.

In the same session, 1928-9, the School took two more steps to improve its conditions of employment for teachers. On the one hand, after lengthy discussions and in agreement with the Professorial Council, the Governors adopted a declaration of policy designed to make sixty-five the normal age of retirement, while preserving their right to require earlier retirement with compensation. On the other hand, they introduced Sabbatical leave; subject to teaching requirements, they planned to give each teacher and administrator once every seven years one term of leave on full pay or two terms on half pay.

The teaching strength of the School grew naturally with its size and number of regular students. The Table of Statistics 1919-37 shows the number of full-time teachers rising from seventeen in the first year [1] to seventy-nine in the last year, that is four times. The regular students in that period had less than doubled, while the occasional students were halved.

Other teachers of the School who may read this book will, I am sure, forgive me if I put a special word here about three teachers who came on to the period of this book from the period before: Cannan and Bowley and Lilian Knowles. I cannot do better than quote from another of Janet's contributions to the *Clare Market Review*. [2]

'Perhaps the best-known of all of the early teachers was

---

[1] The number of seventeen given here for the first year (1919-20) includes seven or eight appointments made during the year, that is after I became Director—on October 1, 1919. The full-time staff before that date as given in *Power and Influence*, p. 170, was itself only seven or eight.

[2] *Early Personalities and Occasions*, C.M.R., Lent Term 1955. All the other early teachers mentioned by Janet in this article (Hobhouse, Wallas, Westermarck, Seligman) also came on to my period and are mentioned elsewhere in this book.

5 *Arnold Plant and Lionel Robbins at Avebury*

6 *Wallas, Ware and Siegfried with others at Avebury*

Professor Edwin Cannan, who came up from Oxford a day or two every week. He was indomitable in keeping to his programme. In the general strike of 1926 he bicycled the fifty miles up to Clare Market. I took him home with me to our house in Campden Hill to spend the night and recover from this amazing feat. He was much loved by students and staff. He had a caustic wit and a very kind heart. Professor Bowley, his contemporary, used also to bicycle to the School from his home before the days of his full-time Chair . . .

'One woman teacher of that time, Lilian Knowles, later Professor of Economic History, will live in the memory of her students not only for her academic distinction, which was high in her field, but for her most sparkling and lovable personality. She had no use for socialism and the labour politics of these days. She was frankly on the side of the Conservatives. When the Director introduced a scheme of family allowances for the Staff of L.S.E., she was strongly against it. She said it was a premium on irresponsibility and pointed to a colleague with five children who would be immensely better off than herself with only one. But everyone liked Lilian Knowles, and enjoyed her gay hats. She was generous in time and devotion to her students.'

One of the happiest moments in my time at the School was in May 1933 when I returned from a visit to Vienna where Lionel Robbins and I had seen the first list of German professors dismissed by Hitler. We had felt at once that action ought to be taken in the School and I wrote to Janet to help in preparing the way. The Professorial Council decided that a rescue fund should be raised by voluntary contributions from the staff taken from their salaries. Almost £1,000 a year was raised in this way for three years, representing nearly two per cent of the salaries, and was spent in providing for displaced German teachers; there came also help volunteered by some Governors. The Academic Assistance Council followed soon after and, when it was established fully, the separate fund of the School became unnecessary. Individual teachers or administrators could and did help through the A.A.C. or its successor S.P.S.L. But it is fair to say that in defence of free learning against tyrants, as in so many other things, the School of Economics was first in the field.

TEACHERS SHOULD RESEARCH

The Founders of the School of Economics and Political Science did not regard teaching as its sole purpose or even as its primary purpose. They wanted to break up economics, to make it something utterly different from before, to advance knowledge by collection and examination of facts. They were not teachers themselves, but researchers.

The Founders' interest in research had probably at least as much to do with their turning the School building as far as possible into a Library, as had their frugal desire to avoid payment of local rates on what they built. They filled the Library with every book and document that they could get into their hands.

The interest of the Founders in advancing knowledge of society by research was carried on fully in the period under review: from 1919 to 1937. Great developments of research took place, and led naturally to making the results of research known by more and more publications of books and of learned periodicals.

In the first School Calendar for which I was responsible, that for 1920-1, I found myself as Director, responsible also for editing seventy monographs by Lecturers and Students of the School, whose mere description filled seven pages of the Calendar. In the last Calendar for which I was responsible, that for 1936-7, the seven pages had become twenty-nine pages.

In addition to this, the list of 165 principal publications (books and articles) issued independently by members of the School Staff filled eight pages. They represented the following principal branches of study: Anthropology and Colonial Administration, Economics (including Banking and Currency, Commerce, and Accounting), Geography, History, International Studies, Law, Modern Languages, Political Science, Psychology, Social Biology, Sociology, Statistics and Transport.

The School publications proper included, in addition to 137 Monographs and Studies, a number of lectures and maps and bibliographies. They included also a few periodical publications, like *Economica* established in January 1921, its companion *Politica* launched in 1934, the *London and Cambridge Economic Service* established in 1922 in co-operation with Harvard, an *Annual Survey of English Law*, and an *Annual Digest of Public International Law*.

They included finally the *New Survey of London Life and Labour*, begun in 1927-8 under charge of Sir Hubert Llewellyn-Smith as a sequel to the famous survey by Charles Booth, and completed six years later in nine volumes at a cost of £21,000.

This completion, recorded in my Report for the session 1933-4, produced a charming final gift and letter of thanks from Mrs. Charles Booth and her son George. The original survey, after all, had employed Beatrice Webb at a critical moment in her life before she met Sidney and may well be regarded as responsible indirectly for their marriage and so for the creation of the School.

The School, in the period under review, did its utmost, by advancing knowledge, to realise the primary aims of its Founders. Except for a small amount spent on unavoidable building, the first of the dollars which it received from Rockefeller sources were used to assist research by teachers of the School, and this use was repeated from time to time.

As is told in another chapter, subject to many other preoccupations as well as my duties as Director, I did what I could both in writing new books, and in bringing old books of mine up to date. I sought also to advance knowledge in a new field of study in which I became interested during my first year as Director, the field of Price and Wage History. I found the Governors of the School very sympathetic to my aim. As an accompaniment to my study of the history of prices and wages in England, parallel studies were started for several European countries—Germany, France, Holland and others. In 1929-30 they allowed me to house International Price History at the School. In June 1934 they gave me leave of absence for two days each week in the Michaelmas and Lent Terms of the coming year. This was their way of meeting my request, becoming by that time rather clamant, to allow me to become a Research Professor rather than Director.[1]

[1] See *Power and Influence*, pp. 248-9.

THE SCHOOL OF ECONOMICS

THE ISSUE OF POLITICAL ACTIVITY

As is told in *Power and Influence*,[1] when Sidney invited me to become Director of the School of Economics, one of the questions which I asked him was whether this post would be compatible with my standing for Parliament. I asked this, not because I had political ambitions, but as a mark of freedom from civil service restrictions. Sidney answered that I should be free to stand, but fortunately no occasion occurred for my standing. I say 'fortunate', because the answer of the Governors of the School to my question was studiously vague; they had just received, or were about to receive, a strong reinforcement of business men interested in the new Commerce Degree, no doubt mainly Conservatives, and at need would probably have answered in the negative.

Laborious search for political activity in all my documents of this time, including the written conversations with my mother where nothing was concealed, has brought to light four examples only for mention here as verging on politics. One was the question put to me in 1922 by my old friend the Provost of Oriel as to whether I would stand with Gilbert Murray to represent the University of Oxford as a Liberal, if the Liberals in the University could find money for election expenses; as they failed to find money or any hope of it, no problem arose for Sidney or myself. Another example was a meeting in Cambridge, at the end of 1922, with a number of 'youngish Liberals (mostly defeated candidates) setting out to discover a policy which should be neither Conservative nor Labour, but mortally afraid of being connected with the existing Liberal organization'. I told my mother that this meeting 'was quite amusing'; I can only hope that the meeting did amuse me, for it involved getting up at 6.30 a.m. next morning, in order to spend the whole of January 1, 1923, in travelling, with three changes of train, to Boothby in Cumberland. My last two examples are shadowy connection for a few years with a 'Liberal Summer School', and drafting in 1924 of a Social Insurance Bill for a Liberal Member to present as propaganda in the House of Commons; Asquith had asked me to do this but Lloyd George objected to the Bill. The rest

[1] pp. 181-2.

of my eighteen years in Houghton Street is silence—politically.

I had not left the Civil Service in order to become a politician. I became absorbed instantly in the work of the School. But, in a few years, three events outside the School made preservation beyond challenge of its claim to be an impartial centre of teaching and research one of its major problems.

One such outside event was the change of political structure in Britain, with the rise of the Labour Party. The subjects mainly taught at the School became more significant than ever before politically. A number of the important teachers in the School were adherents of the Labour Party, as were the Founders of the School. In her Diary for January 29, 1927, Beatrice gives a list of six such teachers—Tawney, Robson, Lloyd, Kingsley Martin, Delisle Burns, Leonard Woolf—full of concern at the low standard of knowledge and thought in the Labour Movement and wanting to start a new political quarterly. Their object, of course, was not so much to organize victory for Labour at the hustings as to use their brains in helping an established victor to be sensible, as I had tried once to help the Liberals to a sensible Bill for Social Insurance. But critics of the School as socialist might not realize what these six teachers were after.

The second outside event was a strike of policemen at Harvard in the United States, which led to yet another teacher of left sympathies joining the staff of the School. Harold Laski, then teaching at Harvard, was thought to have expressed sympathy with the strikers, and had been criticized violently for his attitude. Graham Wallas pleaded with me urgently to rescue him from trouble, and I invited him to come to us, first for half-time and later for full-time. In justice to Harvard and its Principal, I should add my belief that 'rescue' was not needed, and that Lowell would have supported Laski sufficiently; my recollection is that Lowell wrote as much to me at that time. But Laski was with us from October 1920, becoming a well-known public figure, and deepening our red colour in many eyes.

The third outside event was my misfortune in defeating by five votes for the Vice-Chancellorship of London University in June 1926, Sir Ernest Graham Little, M.P. for the University and leader of the External life on its Senate. This defeat made him my enemy and enemy of the School that I was directing; he lost no opportunity of attacking the School as socialist or communist, in letters to the Press and otherwise.

After ten years I began to think that something should be done to bring home to everybody concerned the impartial character of the School. After twelve years, I felt certain of this and I wrote a long memorandum putting the problem. The question was: what could and should be done? As I did always when faced with such general problems, I began by consulting the teachers.

On November 25, 1931, there was a Professorial Council bringing most of the teachers together. I took the opportunity of asking the senior staff to discuss my problem with me. They did so and passed certain resolutions. These were considered almost at once, on December 5th, by the Emergency Committee, which passed resolutions in turn, based on and for the most part the same as those of the senior staff, though with some changes of wording; the Emergency Committee, since 1928, had included three representatives of the Professorial Council. But, before sending their resolutions on to the Governors, the Emergency Committee referred them to the Professorial Council for report.

There followed a riot of discussion, with amendments and counter-amendments, lasting nearly five months. The Professorial Council and Emergency Committee each had two meetings on the problem. But at last there was full agreement, and on May 19, 1932 the full Court of Governors approved the following resolution submitted by Council and Committee together:[1]

'That while members of the staff of the School of Economics should, in the full sense secured to them by Article 28 of the Memorandum and Articles of Association of the School, be free from regulation or censure by the Governors of the School in their writings or public speeches, they should regard it as a personal duty to preserve in such writings or speeches a proper

[1] There were four other resolutions, dealing with such matters as candidature of the staff for Parliament, leave of absence for such a purpose, behaviour while a candidate and so on. For convenience of reference all the resolutions and also Article 28 are printed together in Appendix 2.

regard for the reputation of the School as an academic centre of scientific teaching and research.'

In discussing this resolution, the Council had minuted their view that it was the business of the Director, if it appeared to him that damage was in fact being done to the reputation and interests of the School by the speaking or writing of a colleague, to call the attention of the colleague to this. In passing on to the Professorial Council the Governors' approval of the agreed resolution, I was asked to tell them that the Director would be expected to make a 'light intervention' in case of any infringement of the resolution.

With this resolution of May 1932 accepted by everybody and much in my mind, it seemed to me appropriate in my next Address to New Students to contrast the scientific spirit of not speaking unless one is sure, with the practical reforming spirit of doing something to put a wrong right, even if one was not sure that it was the best thing that could be done. Most of my hearers, I knew, would not go out into the world as scientists but I did hope that all of them, in their years at the School, would gain something of the scientific spirit—of being impartial between disputants till one really knew. I ended with the declaration that 'Members of Parliament cannot be scientific or impartial.'[1]

This was in October 1932. As the Great Depression of the 'thirties deepened, there came a moment, in April 1934, when it seemed to have become my duty to call the attention of one of my colleagues to possible harm that his utterances might be doing to the School. With his reforming spirit Harold Laski, who had succeeded Graham Wallas as Professor of Political Science, was feeling strongly the growing misery of the people, and was giving voice to his feeling.

After I had talked to him, we agreed that I should bring what I felt about some of his utterances before the Emergency Committee of the School, and that I should bring also a connected, though different, point about an arrangement that he had made to write regular articles for the *Daily Herald*. The point here was that the Governors had two distinct scales for professors, one stopping at £1,000 a year and one running to

[1] Much more of this address is printed in *Power and Influence*, pp. 182-3.

£1,250. Their view was that people entitled to this higher figure should not undertake a large amount of outside work also, without asking permission from the Governors and this Laski had not done.

Meeting on July 19, 1934, the Emergency Committee gave it as their opinion 'that the development of public opinion concerning Professor Laski's recent more popular utterances is, in fact, rightly or wrongly against the best interests of the School and ought now to be taken by him into account in deciding on "personal duty" under the Professorial Council Resolution of 1931.'[1] This opinion of the Emergency Committee, with a ruling also that the *Daily Herald* articles represented an outside activity great enough to have required their permission, was sent to me in a letter by Josiah Stamp for transmission to Harold Laski and received an almost immediate reply from him:

"I regard myself as free to make occasional speeches on political topics, especially at such times as a general election. I also regard myself as bound, in making such speeches, by the general sense of the resolution passed by the Professorial Council in 1931.'

He agreed also to stop the *Daily Herald* articles, as from the end of the Long Vacation.

The Emergency Committee expressed on July 27th their appreciation of the way in which Professor Laski had met their views.

*

I have noticed in the chapter before this some of the early addresses given on the annual Oration Day of the School by visiting speakers. For the last such occasion that would occur while I was Director I was invited to make the Oration myself and I did so on June 24, 1937.[2] I made an oration in the special

---

[1] I give the date '1931' as it stands in the Executive Committee minutes. Actually the Professorial Council passed no resolution on this topic before 1932. The 1931 resolution (though practically the same in substance) was that of the Senior Staff.

[2] My Oration is printed in full in *Politica* of September 1937 and there are extracts in Chapter XI of *Power and Influence*. The Oration dealt also with the Method of Social Science and extracts on this subject are given in Chapter VIII below, pp. 94-5.

dictionary sense—of an attempt to persuade in public. I made a plea, to everyone whose business it was to teach or to research in our School, for two things above all—for Observation and for Detachment.

Observation meant basing economics and politics on study of facts and testing by facts, rather than on analysis of concepts—my old quarrel and that of our Founders with the theoreticians.

Detachment meant that University teachers of social science should not be practising politicians. I agreed that, in asking our professors not to be politicians, I was asking them to surrender some of their citizen rights. But I went on to support my plea.

'The civil servant is required to surrender certain citizen rights because, seated at the heart of government, he has so much power to influence its course. The judge makes the same surrender, by custom, if not by rule. The University teacher has been given—often irrevocably—a position of greater trust than that of judge or civil servant. The most precious possession of the community—the ripening mind of adolescence—has been placed in his hand; he has the moulding of the coming generation.

'I do not believe that a University teacher in the Social Sciences can become deeply and personally implicated in political activities and controversies, whether by membership of Parliament or by membership of party organization, whether by writing or by speech, without losing something of his value as a teacher, something of his authority as a scientist.

'The chemist—at least the academic chemist—does not begin an impartial comparison of the properties of leather and rubber by joining the directorate of a tannery . . . '

I said this in 1937. I would not repeat it in those words today.

To begin with, I do not want to detach University teachers from giving good advice on their special subjects to any political party that wants advice, whether they belong to it or not.

To go on with, the British Constitution has a special resource in the House of Lords; if it adds to the persuasiveness of good advice, there is no harm in letting advice come from one who has been made a Peer by a particular party and still adheres to the party, but neither has a vote himself nor as a rule thinks about the votes of other people. Giving advice because it is good is different from helping to organize electoral victory.

To end with, 'Detachment' is a feeble, because negative, word. The right word is 'Dedication'. A University teacher of Social Science should be content with one mistress. He cannot at one and the same time with advantage be a scientist and a practising politician looking for votes, any more than he can with propriety make love to two women at once or marry two wives. But having a wife does not mean that a man must be detached from all friends, and must not advise friends about political issues on which he may feel deeply and have special knowledge. The test whether a teacher wedded to research is flirting too much outside is broadly the test accepted by the L.S.E. Professorial Council in 1932: Is it bringing his proper mistress into disrepute?

To me this means, in practice, that a regular teacher or administrator in a University institution devoted to Social Science should not also hold office of any kind, whether paid or unpaid, in a party political organization for promoting particular social changes. He should resign his University post when he decides to be a practising politician, as Clement Attlee and Hugh Dalton did.

'Dedication'. A priest is dedicate to service of God and to keeping the souls of men alive. A judge is dedicate to justice. A University teacher is dedicate to truth and to youth.

V

ECONOMISTS AT PLAY

BEFORE I came to the School as Director, the athletics of the School were limited practically to mixed hockey, which I also had played but regarded always as unduly dangerous. In my second year, 1920-1, the School rented a playing field of 9 acres at Alperton, but this proved at once too small for our new student body. In 1921 we found a field of 20 acres at Malden, bought it, and built on it, as we could afford and sometimes before we could afford, one pavilion larger and more permanent than the one before.

Malden became an excellent meeting place for students and for teachers—not in professional capacities but as athletes. Both students and teachers, in respect of Malden, owed more than they were allowed to realize at the time to Governors of the School under the influence of Janet.

In another of her *Clare Market Review* articles,[1] for instance, Janet records how, after a Governors' meeting at the School, two Governors drove her home to Campden Hill and she used the opportunity to stress on them the urgent need for more money to spend on Malden. Next morning she found in her post a cheque for £1,000 to be used for Malden, with a condition that the giver's name should be concealed; a little later the same Governor, on appeal from her, gave a first-class eight to the School boat club—on the same condition of anonymity. As, in writing her article, Janet treated the need for anonymity as past, I can give the name here—Eric Miller. I can add that the other Governor, who didn't pour out money on this occasion, was in reality one of the most generous and helpful Governors whom the School has known. Governors generally were only too glad to help the School.

[1] 'Felix Q. Potuit'. *Clare Market Review*, Summer Term 1955.

Malden, for instance, in its early days at a distance from any station, was somewhat inaccessible—a trouble to visiting teams, and to our teams also when they had much equipment. Janet put our trouble to the Governor who was then in charge of London Transport—Frank Pick, and 'tentatively enquired of him whether the London Transport authority had any buses for which they had no particular use'. Janet got the bus at once, from Pick and his Chairman Lord Ashfield, a 'bus sound in itself but about to be superannuated on account of its design'.

'With great rejoicing, the students christened it Jye, which was my name to my own family. Jye, in the purple and the yellow of the School, ran to and from the station for many years.'[1]

Frank Pick on another occasion rendered a much greater service, not to the School directly but to the University of which it was part, in guiding me as Vice-Chancellor to the ideal architect for its Bloomsbury building. Here too he was well advised by Janet.

It may be added that for a short time we organized exercise on the spot rather than by bus, by using three of our Houghton Street rooms for badminton and squash. But this was too good to last for long, in face of the endlessly growing demand for teaching and studying room.

In spite of the novelty of Malden, our teams soon became a force to reckon with by others, and I noted their achievements in inter-collegiate competitions regularly, in my Annual Reports on the work of the School. But only too often I found myself observing that the School had put up teams good enough to win easily, which for some reason had not won. Our first actual success in an inter-collegiate competition came in 1925-6 and was double, in rowing and in chess. In succeeding years, from 1927 to 1932 particularly, the School won three or four inter-collegiate cups each year, with for a time a stranglehold on the Association Football Cup, and was a formidable competitor in most sports. I must admit that one of our normal wins in those days was golf, for which I had presented a cup. As we won this repeatedly, with great ease,

---

[1] The bus also comes into 'Felix Q. Potuit'.

in spite of my being one of the team myself, London University had clearly not learned golf seriously in my time.

During my period, the School at tennis boasted two Wimbledon players, past or present—Mrs. Anstey on the teaching staff and G. P. Hughes as a student. A notable victory for authority was achieved once, when, in a Staff and Student Match, the Director and Mrs. Anstey defeated G. P. Hughes and his partner. The School had another good tennis player in Baron Meyendorff, exiled from Soviet Russia to become Reader in Russian Institutions and Economics in the University of London; he is happily alive today.

Naturally the School plays at Malden still, though it has to use many other places also for the 26 forms of exercise named in the Calendar for 1957-8, from boating to mountaineering and Judo, that are affiliated to its Athletic Union.

*

The Students Union at the School of Economics, in its early days when I studied there myself, was 'a small and very serious body'.[1] After World War I, with its swiftly changing composition and lower age, the student body became less wholly serious. It engaged in forms of athletics less dangerous than mixed hockey. It organized rags. It allowed us to present it with a carved Beaver as a mascot and fellow student. It helped us to raise money for hospitals by Mock Trials. I have dealt with the athletics of the School and its best rag in my period already.[2] I shall say something about the Beaver and the Mock Trials here.

The Beaver came into the life of the School very early in Janet's and my time there, in company with our motto, *Rerum Cognoscere Causas*, as part of a new coat or arms on which he carried two books. I am not quite certain who invented Beaver for us, but I suspect Janet strongly. There is no doubt, as will be told in a moment, that she introduced him to the Students Union and made him a mascot and student himself.

Acquisition of the motto and coat of arms with Beaver was announced formally in my Director's Report of June 24, 1922. The Report proceeded to explanation.

[1] So described in *Power and Influence*, p. 28.
[2] p. 23 for the rag. For Athletics see above, in this chapter.

'It is needless to point out the appropriateness to the School of Economics of an animal of such social habits, so constructive, and gifted with such foresight as is the beaver. The beaver is also reputed to be industrious, though one writer at least has been found to assert that this reputation is undeserved; that "for five long months in winter the beaver does nothing but sleep and eat and keep warm", that "summertime for him is just one long holiday when the beavers are as jolly as grigs with never a thought of work from morning to night" and that in fact he never works at all except in September and October when his dam must be built and when the Final Examinations of the University are held.'

In spite of these doubts raised against the beaver's character, four senior members of the staff proceeded in 1925 to give him as a mascot to the School and to call him Felix. Presentation was made at the Commemoration Dinner introduced two years before as an annual festivity of the School.

The mascot, a finely carved wooden beaver, was brought in covered by a sheet and placed before the Director at table. Professor Dicksee explained that, feeling the need of a mascot for the School, four people—himself and Professor Gutteridge as Deans of the Faculties of Economics and Laws, the Director and the Secretary—had taken steps to meet the need. He called the Secretary to unveil the mascot and she prepared to do so and to christen him 'Felix'.

Thereupon the Director asked Professor Gutteridge to examine Felix on his suitability for admission to read for every degree and diploma in the scope of the School, both as a day and evening student. Satisfied with this examination, Janet unveiled the mascot and handed him to C. E. Maggs, President of the Students Union as his Advisor of Studies:

'Will you, Felix's advisor of studies, undertake to teach him the whole duty of a student of this School, seeing to it that he is never absent from any inter-collegiate contest, whether of football, rowing or cricket?

'Will you see that he attends all the meals served in the refectory, whether of a routine or festive nature, and that he never smokes on the stairs?

'Will you see that he also attends all the lectures he is expected to attend?

"Will you protect him from the predatory visits of our friends from Gower Street, the Strand, Exhibition Road and any other part of London where University degrees are sought?

'And will you, above all, make it your especial care that he neither fosters nor stands for any but the finest traditions of University life in School and in this country?'

Round the basis of the beaver was carved the line of Virgil from which the School motto is derived: *Felix qui potuit rerum cognoscere causas.* In the past, Latin scholars had been wont to translate that line: 'Happy he could understand the causes of things.' But a new class of scholars, steeped in the dog Latin of the Middle Ages, had risen to assert a different meaning: 'It is only Felix who can understand the causes of things.' Ability to understand things is no doubt the reason which brought Felix to the School.

★

The School of Economics, between the wars, gave itself to plenty of cheerful nonsense with brains behind it. The next piece of nonsense to be noticed here had the justification of raising money for a good cause. As soon as the building begun by the King in 1920 had been completed, the organizers of King Edward's Hospital Fund realized the chance of publicity and a little money that the theatre of new School of Economics in the traffic heart of London gave them.

They organized from 1923 to 1931 a variety of lectures and counter-lectures, biographical duets, cross-examinations and indictments, in which nearly every well-known journalist, actor, not-too-serious professor or author was asked to play the fool for a good cause.

They went on to three years of Mock Trials in which every not-too-serious occupation, from actresses, airmen and biographers to the ballet or 'The Young' was assaulted.

I have written already something about three of these Mock Trials,[1] and return briefly to them now with some new nonsense.

[1] *Power and Influence*, pp. 228-33. The account given there, covering five and a half large pages is much longer than what is printed here and is not repeated. I have added only a few unpublished gems of nonsense.

In the first of these three trials I was a criminal. Economists, including myself with Hubert Henderson, Theodore Gregory, and Arthur Salter, were charged with 'Conspiring to Create Mental Fog and Confusion'.

In the return match against the Politicians a year later, I prosecuted. Politicians were charged with practising unnatural and diabolical arts, 'whereby you have contrived to keep your ears at all times close to the ground, while at the same and all other times having your heads in the air, and your hands in the pockets of the people'. The politicians called on to answer this charge included Lady Astor, Robert Boothby, Gwilym Lloyd George, James Maxton and John Wallace.

A year later, I prosecuted again, charging the Ancient Greeks with the crime of Not Knowing that They are Dead. The nonsense here covered a serious difference of opinion, as to the value of classical studies, between myself and two very distinguished defendants—T. R. Glover, then Public Orator at Cambridge, and Cyril Norwood, just become President of St. John's College, Oxford. I had the slightly unfair advantage of having spent nine years of my life at school and at Oxford in studying the Classics, and I gave a list of things said about women by the Ancient Greeks which deprived them of all hope of kindness from a modern audience largely female. My examples of what the Ancient Greeks thought of women began with the doctrine of Hypereides:

'No woman ought to go outside her house till she is of age to make passers-by ask not whose wife she is but whose mother she is.'

They ended with Aristotle's view of femaleness as a 'kind of physical defect' and Plato's elaboration:

'Of the men who came into the world, those who were cowards or led unrighteous lives may be supposed to have changed into the nature of women in the second generation.'

Under the judgeship of J. A. Spender, the defendants were ordered to drink hemlock, did so, and lay dead. As soon as the stretcher-bearers came to bear the corpses away, they rose up and left the stage among cheers.

The whole of this nonsense from 1933 to 1936, makes more cheerful reading than can be found easily today. And it raised nearly £5,000 for the Hospitals.

7   *Edwin Cannan, 1920*

8 *Lilian Knowles, Professor of Economic History, 1921-6*

VI

PRE-OCCUPATIONS OF A DIRECTOR

WHEN I accepted the Directorship of the School, Sidney assured me that I should have plenty of time for economic research and writing. MacKinder had run the School 'with two fingers of one hand'. I should be able to write one, two, as many books as I wanted, as quickly as I wanted. Things did not work out as Sidney forecast.

In my eighteen years as Director I published two substantial books only—*British Food Control* in 1929 and an enlarged edition of *Unemployment : A Problem of Industry* a year later. In 1929 and again in 1934 I made determined attempts to exchange the Directorship for a Professorship at the School, in which I could do research that would lead to books.

Two things have to be admitted in defence of Sidney's forecast. First, I did write quite a lot of booklets, pamphlets, articles and addresses; bound as *Varia* they form two stout volumes on my shelves today. Second, my difficulty in getting books written was not due solely to my work as Director. I was doing many other things as well continually.

I cannot show this better than by extracts from letters which I wrote to my mother in October and November 1925, from three different addresses, at a time when she was pressing to return from her country house on Hindhead to the house in Campden House Road where she and my father had lived with me since the end of 1921.

October 30, 1925.   *53 Campden House Road, W.8.*
'The Coal Commission and the School and servants have left me with literally no crack of time this week. So you'll understand my not writing before . . .

Meanwhile I'm frantically busy, with one or two important School things added to the C.C. Yesterday also I added luncheon with "my Crown Prince". There was a distinguished company, as you'll see by today's *Times*, and I found myself seated next to the Prime Minister and next but one to the Crown Prince. The latter was very pleasant and quite young and talked about the efforts made by Sweden to do without coal and use water-power. I said something to the P.M. about his "dreadful" subsidy to coal, and corrected it to "excellent" subsidy. He begged me to keep the first adjective, as much the truer one!'

Royal Commission on the Coal Industry (1925).
2 Queen Anne's Gate Buildings,
Dartmouth Street,
October 30, 1925.   Westminster, S.W.1.
'I am most anxious to make it possible for you to return to London as soon as possible, and but for my pre-occupations with Coal should certainly have been able to find suitable servants before now . . .
I'll write again tonight after seeing (as I hope) my latest candidate.'

The London School of Economics and Political Science.
(University of London).
Houghton Street,
November 19, 1925.   Aldwych, W.C.2.
'I have just seen a cook-housekeeper—by name Miss Anthony—with 11 years character, who wishes to come to me and promises very well indeed . . .
If I now concentrate on getting a house parlour-maid I am sure that I ought to be able to manage it . . .
Coal Commission continues to be very absorbing.'

I am glad to resurrect these three letters, with their apparently justified confidence that, in the intervals of settling difficulties at the School of Economics and sitting on a Royal Commission, I could find a cook and a housekeeper. What a ridiculously easy life intellectuals had thirty-four years ago! The second of these letters has suggested the title which seems to fit the present chapter best: *Pre-occupations* of a Director. Between them, the letters illustrate three such pre-occupations—public service such as that on the Coal Commission. the social life of public and private entertainment, and care of parents. Three other pre-occupations for me were scouring the country by motor, walking up mountains, and writing books. These six pre-occupations, added to the Directorship, made a very full life indeed. In a written conversation with my mother, just before I sailed for America in December 1926, I ended by saying: 'I wish there were three of me. One to go to America and the others to be here with you and H.B.'[1] 'Three of me' seems to me now an understatement of the need.

A few words will be said about each of my pre-occupations; the last three generally, though not invariably, went together and are dealt with together, under a comprehensive title, as 'Motors, Mountains and Manuscripts'.

PUBLIC SERVICE

Till the moment when I became Director, I had been engaged as a Civil Servant for ten years on a great variety of work and had gained experience which others than myself might think valuable. When I received Sidney's invitation to become Director, I consulted naturally Hubert Llewellyn Smith, head of the Board of Trade to which I still belonged officially, as to whether the Board seemed likely to have need of me. His answer was that the Board seemed unlikely to want me badly enough to justify me in refusing an offer so attractive as Sidney's. but that in accepting the offer, if I did so, I should stipulate that I might be free to help the Government in any general economic enquiries that might be necessary.[2] As it happened, early in my time as Director, in July 1921, there did come a Government request for my service in economic enquiry: I was asked to go to India as Vice-President of a Commission on Tariff Policy. This, in spite of its attraction

[1] My mother was still living with me in Kensington and my father had gone back to Hindhead.

[2] Reflecting on this letter afterwards, I have at times wondered why the Government should feel entitled to call on my service and experience, while refusing me any pension whatever for the ten years of hard work that I have done for them as a Civil Servant (*Power and Influence*, p. 160). Llewellyn Smith, of course, had nothing to do with this refusal.

for me, with my Indian connection, I felt bound, after consultation with Sidney, to decline.

But, even before this invitation to India, came another call
for service arising out of my previous work, which I did not
feel able to refuse. One of the last and most moving of my
experiences as a Civil Servant had been the visit which I paid
to Austria, Czecho-slovakia and Hungary in January 1919 as
British member of an Inter-Allied Commission to discover
how war had left these countries. This had led to a troubled
week at Versailles where I had endeavoured vainly to convince
Lloyd-George and the other leaders of the victorious nations,
that Vienna was starving and freezing and that for Austria,
at least, our policy should be rescue rather than demand for
reparations. Janet, as an official of the Ministry of Food, was
there as well.

My move from the Civil Service to the School gave me both
freedom of speech on Austria and a way to practical help. At
the very beginning of my time as Director, in January 1920, I
dashed off to Vienna again, returning to urge remedial action
on my friends still in the Civil Service, like John Bradbury
and Basil Blackett, and to publish a pamphlet on *Peace in
Austria*. The practical help took the form of organizing, with
support, of course, from School teachers and the University
of Vienna, a series of University Summer Courses there, that
might make the Viennese feel themselves to be part of the
civilized world again and bring a little money into the place.
These courses, begun in 1922, have continued to the present
day, subject only to war interruption.

There followed for me a succession of public activities such
as the British Association meetings at Liverpool in 1923 and
Toronto in 1924, at each of which I had to read papers; the
Coal Commission of 1925-6; the Vice-Chancellorship of the
University of London involving the battle for Bloomsbury in
1926-8; the Academic Assistance Council of 1933 carried on by
the Society for Protection of Science and Learning to the
present day;[1] the Unemployment Insurance Statutory Committee from 1934 to 1944. Chairmanship of this Committee
carried a salary of £1,000 a year; so I told the Governors that

[1] Described by me in *A Defence of Free Learning* published by the
Oxford University Press in June 1959.

I could not accept the post unless they cut my salary as Director by the same amount, and they did so. This seemed to me right in principle and had the advantage of helping the finance of the School at a difficult moment. This Chairmanship did not take much of my time, but was all up my street and very interesting. I was also, for six months in 1936, Chairman of a Committee to advise the Government on Rationing Machinery in case war came again; I can only hope that the advice of the Committee proved of some use when war did come.

SOCIAL LIFE

The social life of the 1920's was very full, even for economists. In June 1921 I found myself apologizing to my mother for not writing to her, giving as excuse that this was my busy season at the School in preparing the programme and calendar for the coming year—'and in one way or another I seem to have been occupied most evenings as well'.

'On Tuesday, J. S. Nicholson (of the Labour Exchanges), having seen his family off to the country, took me and others to dine and see the Russian Ballet, which was just as attractive as ever; on Wednesday I went with another party to a foolish Revue; on Thursday to a dining club, chiefly of shipowners to whom I discoursed on Unemployment; on Friday to dinner with Dr. Savill (a distinguished woman doctor) to meet Captain Elliott, M.P., talk about coal mines; yesterday, being my one chance, to Wimbledon where I saw some quite amazing lawn tennis; today I was to have gone to tennis at Highgate with Lees Smith (one of our lecturers) and his belongings, but was stopped by a tragedy—his father having been found dead in his bath—choked by gas from a geyser apparently. So I spent the time in catching up arrears of work on the School Calendar and on an *Encyclopaedia Britannica* article on Rationing.

'I've another very busy week ahead, ending up with a visit of Empire University Professors to the School on Friday and to Dunford House at the weekend. One of them will be stopping with me here from Thursday onward . . . '

Apart from this sometimes frivolous entertainment, I was constantly meeting interesting people, who seemed worth reporting to my mother.

In August 1923, when I was staying at Callander with David and Janet and their family (with a view, for me, of climbing mountains), Janet and I went over to lunch with Haldane and see his mother at 98 years of age. Haldane seized the chance to talk to me about the University of London and the law.

In June 1924, I reported to her what Mrs. Robert Lynd had said about conversations between Lloyd George and myself:

'She told me that I had contradicted Lloyd George and made him cry. I said, "What nonsense." "That is just what you are reported to have said." '

I was, in fact, at that moment a good deal in disagreement with Lloyd George about social insurance. I had drafted, at Asquith's request, a Social Insurance Bill for a Liberal member to introduce as propaganda, and Lloyd George had broken in with something I didn't like, bringing in the Prudential and other Industrial Assurance companies.

In 1925 came a meeting with Tibetan Lamas, just how organized I do not know, but duly written out for my mother. 'I never told you about the Tibetan Lamas whom I saw on Thursday night. The reception was in a large high studio, with the Lamas sitting on a dais in an alcove at one end. Three of them, with attendants.

Each of us went up and gave his name and description to an introducer (who was one of the Everest expedition) who passed it on to a Tibetan interpreter who interpreted. (But there was no Tibetan word for "Economics".)

Then one shook hands and gave one's present. If the Chief Lama liked it, he kept it himself. Otherwise he passed it on to one of his juniors. He passed on mine which didn't interest him. A clockwork toy gave him most joy!

We saw also the porter who built the camp for Mallory and Irvine at 27,000 feet up. An amazing feat, to carry up all the materials and provisions.

The pleasant thing was that we were just as much a show to them as they to us.

Later they chanted to us in Tibetan.'

I tried even to learn golf, explaining to my mother once

that 'it's the only thing that really takes meteorology out of my mind'.[1]

This list of meetings, conversations and frivolities could be multiplied indefinitely.

CARE OF PARENTS

My father, Henry Beveridge, born in February 1837, was nearer to eighty-three than eighty-two when I became Director of the School. My mother, Annette, was nearing seventy-seven. Each had nearly ten years to live. My mother had suffered from defective hearing for many years and for the past seven years had become so deaf that all conversation with her had to be written down.

They had met and married and spent their normal working lives in India, where all their children had been born. On return to Britain they had by no means lost their interest in India. Each had become an excellent Oriental Scholar, studying the history and literature of the Mogul Empire from Babur to Akbar in the original Turki and Persian. This meant that, while living since 1894 on Hindhead, Surrey, in a small country house called Pitfold, they needed to visit London frequently, to study in the Oriental room of the British Museum or in the India Office. They could and did stay with me whenever they wanted, in the small house which I occupied at 27 Bedford Gardens in Kensington, but it was not large enough to be comfortable for long. By 1919 they were beginning to find both the journeys between Haslemere and London, and the care and staffing of Pitfold burdensome.

So, early in May 1921, having got the chance of a larger house whose lease I could buy at 53 Campden House Road, I invited my parents to come and live with me there, in rooms and with furniture of their own, and they did so for several years. As has been shown in the letters cited already from October and November 1925, I had at that time servant troubles, but with the help at need of Janet I generally overcame them.

[1] See p. 76 below for explanation of why meteorology was in my mind. My conversations of May 1920 with my mother are concentrated on my discoveries of periodicity in the weather and on the statistics that I was doing about it 'in my bed'.

My father, however, in that same year 1925, having ended his Oriental studies some years before, decided that it was his duty at the age of 88 to live at Pitfold and look after it; my mother followed him there two years later at 85. Having still my excellent housekeeper and parlour-maid I was able to help my parents out by persuading one or other of these to look after them at Pitfold, particularly when I was away from London. But by 1927, even when free of urgent School problems, I was apt to be busy either with the Bloomsbury site or with starting my new edition of *Unemployment: a Problem of Industry* or both.

'I am afraid Pitfold is getting to be rather a burden. Perhaps when Bloomsbury is settled I shall have leisure to help you with it.'

So I wrote to my mother in April 1927 from Hale in Cheshire where I was staying with Kenneth Lee, my colleague of the Coal Commission.

'I hope all goes well with you. I had a note from Dora (house parlour-maid) saying she was going to Pitfold on the 5th and another from Miss Anthony (cook-housekeeper) on her return to London. She said she had had a very pleasant time at Pitfold.'

So I wrote to my mother on September 8, 1927, from Dinnet in Aberdeenshire, where with John Fulton, newly come from Balliol to L.S.E., I was working at *Unemployment* in the intervals of climbing nearly all the Cairngorms.

There came at last a moment when even my mother and my father had to be taken in hand—not merely helped to go their own ways.

My mother, in the autumn of 1928, fell ill and was taken to a nursing home near Haslemere. As I could not be with her there, I brought her up to a London home. But in March 1929, at well past 86, she died.

My father I brought to the care of my excellent staff in Kensington, and he died in my house in November 1929, half-way between 92 and 93.

So my parents came to their ends in my personal care. I owe this essentially to the untiring help that Janet gave me, both in finding staff and in every other way at that moment.

Today, as we all know, care of parents is even harder than it was thirty years ago.

The year of my mother's death was the year also when I made the first of my attempts to abandon the Directorship of the School, in order to become a Professor, with more time for research and writing.[1] The double event produced for me one of the longest of many charming letters that I received from Beatrice Webb.

April 5th.

'My dear Sir William,

Sidney and I were very gratified by your two visits here—it is pleasant that you like talking to the old Webbs. This is one reason for our not being keen about your ceasing to be Director—no other Director would treat us so well as you have done!

We both sympathize with your desire to do constructive thinking while you are still in the prime of life—and certainly economics is a vitally necessary science at the present time. But whether you can get a Director of sufficient standing to take your place is a difficult question—Salter would of course do admirably. I seem to remember that someone told me some time ago that his interests now were almost exclusively Foreign Affairs and that he would like to be closely connected with Diplomacy? I may either have misunderstood, or my informant may not have known. And there may be other men equally suited.

However, I don't feel that the question is urgent. You have had a great shock in your mother's death—the loss of a life-long companionship—and you will see more clearly the alternatives before you when you have recovered from it . . .
Always yours affectionately.'

MOTORS, MOUNTAINS AND MANUSCRIPTS

I had bought my first car in 1909, I had climbed my first mountain—Helvellyn—as a boy, and I had begun producing manuscript for a living in 1905. Now that war and the Civil

---

[1] This attempt is described in *Power and Influence*, pp. 247-8, with two sentences only of Beatrice's letter. The bulk of the letter is published now for the first time.

Service for me were over, these three occupations made an overpowering call, which I answered as fully as my other tasks allowed. I have told something of this already in *Power and Influence*.[1] I add here one or two incidents not recorded there, illustrating respectively my dealings with my mother and the conditions under which in those years I wrote books. A feature common to most of my careerings about Britain then was that they started at 3 a.m. in the morning, except when they started at 2 a.m.

In August 1923, for instance, having dropped my sister for some reason at the foot of a Welsh mountain, I whirled myself or was whirled by way of Langdale in the Lakes (night spent with the Trevelyans) to Callander in Perthshire (starting at 2 a.m. on this occasion) for a short holiday with Janet and all her family. Thence, after climbing two mountains 'with fine views' and lunching with Haldane to meet his mother, I dashed South on September 6th to pick up my mother and sister for a motor tour in Wales, to be completed before I was due for the British Association meeting at Liverpool on September 12th.

This Welsh trip included the journey from Llanidloes to Machynlleth, which in those days was described in a cycling guide as 'a quite impracticable road. It consists of a series of precipitous hills utterly unrideable up and highly dangerous down'. My comment at the time was that the road deserved this description. 'I have a vivid memory of one or two head-long slopes down which we looked in the fading light before descending them in bottom gear.' My mother never turned a hair; then and always she was without fear.

In September 1926 I disappeared with Philip Mair to Dalry in Kirkcudbrightshire and got on with my first book as Director, on *British Food Control*.

September 6, 1926.   The Lochinvar Hotel,
                                                    Dalry,
                                                    Kirkcudbrightshire.
'I've just had two days of solid writing (or rather revising) up to 2 a.m. last night and all day today. But before that Phil and I had one day of absolutely glorious expeditioning. We

[1] pp. 215-6.

74

got up at 4.30 a.m., motored eight miles in the light of a waning moon and misty dawn to an upland farm, and walked two and a quarter hours, first across a high pass, then down into a great trough of morass between two mountain ranges (the notorious Cooran Lane which is said to be impassable in many places) and across it, wet but without risk of being bogged, to the three utterly remote lochs—Long Loch of Dungeon, Round Loch of Dungeon and Dry Loch—which were our objectives, lying just below the Dungeon Hill which used to be the resort of all the evildoers in these parts. All this with the sun rising behind us on a perfect day and the mists floating away from the mountains in front. At the lochs we stayed from 8 a.m. to 6 p.m. fishing and sleeping in the sun and eating, and returned in the sunset over the summit of the range which we had crossed by a pass in the morning, to our car again and so here by 9 p.m.—a sixteen-hour day of open air (but not too much exercise) and incredible charm of desolate mountains.

I've three more days here and hope to give one to going back to those lochs, and one to two others, not quite so remote.

Of course, my dear mother, you'll think I ought to think of and desire other things than books and mountains, and I most certainly do, but at least these particular things are good.'

In September 1927 I did the same kind of thing with a different companion, to get on with the new edition of *Unemployment*.

September 8, 1927.   Headinch,
                                          Dinnet,
                                          Aberdeenshire.

I arrived here on Monday and am comfortably settled with Fulton in a farmhouse about three miles from Ballater on the south side of the Dee. We are about 800 feet up and have thus excellent air which compels an inordinate amount of sleep.

Yesterday and the day before the weather has been mainly bad—so that we have done a lot of reading about Unemployment. I am getting to work on the new Edition, and I want Fulton—who is of Balliol just come to the School as an assistant—to take up some aspect of that problem for his own research. Unfortunately a box of books which should have left Liphook more than a week ago hasn't arrived yet so I'm rather spinning cobwebs in the air. But the new edition, or rather the addition to the old edition, *Unemployment Twenty Years After* is taking good shape in my mind.

We shan't, however, devote ourselves wholly to work and with the car have plans for ascending the Cairngorm mountains and Lochnagar. Last night the weather relented and after tea we had a fine walk up a hill just behind the house—2,000 feet high—and got a view of the whole length of the Dee Valley and of some at least of the Cairngorms ... '

We seem, in fact, on this occasion to have climbed most of the Cairngorms, in pursuit, no doubt, of the ambition I had once of ascending every height of more than 3,000 feet in Scotland, or more than 2,500 feet in England.

Expeditions such as these to Dalry or Dinnet were my adaptation of *The Bothie of Tober-Na Vuolich*, a poem by a Balliol predecessor which I have possessed and loved since my Balliol days. I combined the mental and physical activities of Clough's heroes to the full, and gloated over the mountain names as Clough does, though I did not meet an Elspie of the Bothie and take her to New Zealand. My mother was always hoping that I would marry that way, if in no other way.

I suspect that these holidays had something to do with the growing urgency of my requests from 1929 onwards to find an easier life for research and authorship. In addition to the subjects like unemployment, social insurance, and food control which had interested me before, I had acquired in my first year of all at the School an absorbing new topic—Price and Wage History, both for its own sake and as destined, incidentally, to demonstrate periodicity in the weather. I had found in Hubert Hall the best possible colleague to help me in making a new history of Prices and Wages, from material far richer than anything available to my predecessor Thorold Rogers. I had collected enough money in various ways to get together a strong team of other helpers. Here was a tremendous piece of research crying to be done, an indispensable addition to economic and social history, whether or not my theories of periodicity in the weather proved to be meteorology or moonshine. But it could not be done by me while I carried also the responsibilities of Director of the London School of Economics.

Having mentioned this topic, as explaining some of my actions twenty to thirty years ago, I hope I may be allowed to look forward for a moment now. I did, on leaving London for Oxford, contrive to get published a first rather stolid volume on Price History, with intention of proceeding to two or three more volumes, but that was in 1936, after which one new task after another came to me as to others. I can say now only that the magnificent material which Hubert Hall and others gathered, particularly on wages from about 1200 to 1800, and which has been partly worked on, is still available. It will need more and younger brains than mine to reap the harvest. But once the book that I am writing at this moment is finished, I should regard making the largest contribution that I can to the reaping of this harvest my principal task, till I end.

VII

THE PROBLEM OF
ACADEMIC SELF-GOVERNMENT

THE School of Economics was described once by a University
Committee of Inspection as having been a 'benevolent autocracy'. I have never discovered what period of the School's
history they had in mind; it certainly did not fit anything that
happened in my time there. For some purposes the School
when I first became Director might have been described as a
one-woman show, with no Director for the past four months
and with Miss Mactaggart, a highly efficient and experienced
Secretary and Dean, managing all the material side of the
School and admitting students. But of course she could not be
an autocrat to the teachers.

The real weakness of the School at that moment was that
there were hardly any full-time teachers of much standing [1]
and the part-timers forming most of the teaching staff took
little or no part in School affairs beyond giving their lectures.
They could hardly do anything except lecture or read in the
library, because there were practically no private rooms for
teachers. The Professorial Council of twenty met only twice
each year, at the beginning and end of each session. Till the
year of my appointment, when three members of the Council
were given seats on the Court of Governors,[2] no teachers had
any occasion to meet any Governors.

All this seemed to me contrary to the way in which a
University institution should be managed that I set myself to

[1] The only full-time professors were A. L. Bowley and A. J. Sargent
whose appointment as such at the new scale of £1,000 a year I had
proposed and secured in the interval between accepting the Directorship
in June 1919 and taking it up on October 1st.

[2] The Calendar for 1920-21 shows as Governors Prof. Cannan, Dr. Lilian
Knowles and Prof. Sargent.

remedy it as fast as I could. In my first month as Director, as I have told in Chapter I, I asked the Professorial Council to appoint an Office Committee to advise me on administrative matters with an academic bearing; such matters included, among other things, allocation of fees, allocation of rooms, and admission of students. In July 1921 three larger changes came: an Appointments Committee of the Professorial Council was established to advise the Director on all appointments to the regular teaching staff or important changes in the status of teachers; the Library Committee was to include always three members of the teaching staff; the Professorial Council was to meet twice a term in place of twice a year.

These steps towards increasing the responsibility of the teachers and diminishing the power of the Director were taken with my full consent—indeed on my initiative. And they were carried further by me continually. At or immediately after the setting up of the Appointments Committee in July 1921, I undertook not to depart from the advice of the Committee without reference to the Governors. Two years later, as is told just below, the Director's power of appointment was made still less, again with my full assent.

The practical refutation of any idea that the School was an autocracy after I came there lies in the fact that the answer in 1925 to the University Inspectors who called it an autocracy was drafted by a committee of our Professorial Council, and was approved by the Governors without change except acceptance of a few amendments proposed by Professor Hobhouse, then one of the Council's representatives on the Court. It may be added that this answer included the statement that it had 'always been recognized both by the Court of Governors and by successive Directors that anything in the nature of an autocracy is incompatible with the character of a great University institution'.

Having made the teachers more active in administration, I did the same for the Governors. I persuaded them in November 1912 to set up a small Emergency Committee for what was in fact an emergency at that moment—concerned with acquisition of houses. But the Emergency Committee, once established, became in practice the Governing body of the School, kept small enough for real discussion. In 1925 its total of ten included two representatives of the Professorial Council; in 1928 these representatives were increased to three.

While increasing continually the responsibilities of others, I accepted readily cutting down of the complete delegation of power from the Governors that had once belonged to me.

Early in 1923, for instance, the Governors set up a Committee 'to consider what steps could be taken to dissipate the view held in some quarters that the School is being used for partisan propaganda'. The step that they took, on my suggestion, was to limit the Director's power of making appointments even with the consent of the Appointments Committee. The Director in future should be able to make probationary appointments for not more than two years: anything after that or longer than that would require confirmation by the Governors.

Ten years later, in 1933-4, came the student troubles described in Chapter III. With my full assent again, power of expulsion of a student or his suspension for more than three months was taken away from the Director and was given to a Board of Discipline on which he would sit with two representatives of the Governors and two of the Professorial Council—five in all.

All these changes and many others were described by me in a memorandum of Reflections on the School of Economics which I wrote and circulated in the autumn of 1935. In addition to showing how the constitution of the School of Economics was built up piecemeal by decisions on practical problems, as the British Constitution and the Common Law had been built, the memorandum makes several points which I still find interesting.

First comes an admission of 'the somewhat cautious policy which, in my early days at the School, I felt it desirable to adopt towards the Governors'. On the introduction of the Commerce Degree the University Senate had added nine business men to our Governors—'a new and at that time unknown element'; my Oxford life had inclined me to believe that a University institution should be governed from within rather than from without. It is hardly needless to say that caution towards the new Governors disappeared very soon in friendship.

9   *Staff v. Students match at Malden, c. 1926*

10 *Interior of the Cobden Library*

Second, comes recognition of the opposite danger—of leaving too much to those already at work in a learned institution.

'To leave a decision whether some new development should or should not be adopted to the vote of a body of specialists in studies already established, is likely to be fatal to progress. If the growth of the London School of Economics had depended on a vote of the Academic Council of the University of London, deciding to allocate to Economics, or Politics, or Sociology funds which might have fed the offspring of mathematicians or philologists or chemists, the School of Economics would have died at birth. The same argument applies to possible new developments in the School of Economics itself and additions to its former scope.'

The complete autonomy of the colleges of Oxford and Cambridge is not regarded by most observers as making the colleges the mainspring of change and progress in those ancient Universities.

Third, comes emphasis on two points presenting special problems in the government of the School of Economics. One point is the importance attached by its Founders to research rather than to teaching, the resulting high proportion of post-graduate work, and the problem of relation between graduates and post-graduates. The other point, is the close relation between all the different subjects taught at the School. It is not divided naturally into distinct departments. I should be interested to know how far these differences from other Colleges present problems as to its best government today, now that it is so large.

I had not come to the School of Economics in 1919 for power. I valued the initiative which my position as Director gave me, for at the age of forty I thought myself still accessible to new ideas. But I sought to exercise initiative by persuasion only. The measure which in the end caused so much controversy—establishment of a Chair of Social Biology—was approved unanimously by the Professorial Council after full discussion, before the School was committed to it in any way.

I pursued academic self-government for the School of Economics unremittingly. A University which is not self-governing is not a University at all. But to this thesis two riders must be added.

First, self-government does not imply disregard for the views of others. Self-governing Universities, like self-governing nations, are not in the world alone and are not there for their own amusement. They must have organs for keeping in touch with outside opinion and discussing it seriously. On the whole, the various organs—of Governors, Professorial Council, Emergency Committee, Appointments Committee, Students Union and the rest which we built up step by step in the School— seem to me still to have been reasonably satisfactory for this purpose, for an institution of our special character, in the University of London.

Second, self-government, while it is a condition of life for a University, is not its purpose. What the world needs from University teachers and scholars of genius is not that they should spend their time on administration and committees. The world needs, from all who can do it, that they should discover the truth and advance knowledge in their own fields and should teach and inspire the young. Those are the essential tasks of the academic staff of a University. The function of the administrative staff, as I put it once on behalf of Janet and myself at the School, is not that of getting its own way, but that of setting the academic staff free for what it alone can do.

VIII

THE SCOPE AND METHOD
OF SOCIAL SCIENCE

THE Founders of the School, though they started it with practically no money, set no limit to their ambitions; they drew their circle wide. 'The London School of Economics and Political Science,' as I have put it elsewhere, 'was always mis-described in its title; from its beginning it included, not economics and political science alone, but statistics, sociology, geography and several branches of law; anthropology was added in 1903.' When I came to the School as Director, 'I pursued this Webb idea to its logical conclusion; the London School of Economics ought to be a School of all the Social Sciences.'[1]

The Founders of the School had definite ideas also as to the methods by which Social Science should be pursued. They wanted to base economics, politics and all the other social sciences on collection and examination of facts rather than on analysis of concepts; they wanted, in effect, to see applied to the study of human society the methods by which natural scientists had won their many triumphs in discovering the secrets of nature.

I shall deal first with the question of scope, second and more briefly with that of method.

SCOPE OF SOCIAL SCIENCE

My first practical step for widening our scope lay in strengthening greatly the legal side of the School. I contrived in 1920 to get one of the posts on the Cassel Foundation made into a Chair of Commercial and Industrial Law. The holder,

[1] *Power and Influence*, p. 176.

H. C. Gutteridge, proved invaluable in many more ways than one.[1]

Three years later I contrived a Chair of English Law—the first full-time Professorship of Law in the University of London. It was a delight to me to persuade my former teacher of Oxford—Edward Jenks—to leave the Law Society and become first occupant of our Chair. On him followed several younger teachers. The School became very strong in Law; in co-operation with the two other Colleges concerned (University and King's) we were able for the first time to arrange a full day course for Law degrees in London.

It is interesting to know from the Memoirs of Hugh Dalton, who was teaching in the School at this time and before it, that both the senior teachers with whom he worked there—Edwin Cannan and H. S. Foxwell—emphasized the need for economists to know some law. This, he writes, was a favourite theme with each of them.[2]

From Law I found myself turning unexpectedly to an altogether different field for enlarging the scope of the School. In September 1923, while, as President of the Economic Section of the British Association, I was controverting at Liverpool with Maynard Keynes and Marie Stopes on *Population and Unemployment*, there arrived in London Beardsley Ruml, representing the Laura Spelman Rockefeller Memorial.[3] He was clearly looking for objects worthy of help with dollars, came to see me at Liverpool, and on our return to London, came to dine with Sidney Webb and myself. I never left Sidney out of any such affairs, both because he was so useful, and because he deserved to be in on anything important for the School.[4] Ruml had to leave at the end of

[1] Among other things, he discovered the Malden Field for athletics in 1921, he wrote in 1924 a memorandum on Private Bill legislation which helped materially to victory in the Battle of Houghton Street, and he helped to bring the mascot Felix into being in 1925.

[2] *Call Back Yesterday* by Hugh Dalton, p. 113.

[3] The Memorial had been established by John D. Rockefeller on the death of his wife Laura Spelman with a view to commemorating her. It was distinct from the Rockefeller Foundation, had been given very large resources and was intended to do something distinctive. Later it was absorbed into the Rockefeller Foundation.

[4] A few months later, in May 1924, Colonel Arthur Woods, acting President of the Laura Spelman Rockefeller Memorial, happened to be in London and I naturally arranged a dinner for him also, with Sidney in the House of Commons.

September for New York, but took with him a memorandum by myself on two urgent needs, which at the turn of the year, led to grants for building and for economic research.

These immediate grants amounted to nearly $100,000, but there was much more behind. Janet, on a telegram from me, had broken her holiday with children at Callander in Scotland and come to Liverpool for a talk with Ruml. She was the first to talk to him, and he was looking for something big and new. The Natural Bases of the Social Sciences, the theme in effect of my first Address at the School, on 'Economics as a Liberal Education' began to be bruited. That was in accord with my personal interest, as it was in accord with Beatrice's desire for biology as a preliminary to economic studies. But it was far too important for me to do anything effectively about it without carrying with me the teachers of the School.

There developed an interesting difference of priorities, as between Beardsley Ruml and myself, as to where money was most needed. He was attracted immensely by the idea of promoting study of the Natural Bases of the Social Sciences. But though I wanted that extension of our scope, I knew well that there were several other things for which money was indispensable to us at once. We needed another £20,000 for development of the Houghton Street houses just acquired, £8,000 in the Library for binding and a subject catalogue, and above all, endowment of a full-time Chair of Political Economy. Edwin Cannan, our invaluable part-time professor for so many years, was about to retire. We must be in a position to lure the most distinguished economist anywhere to come to us. It became obvious, in discussion with Ruml, that the School would have a far better chance of dollars for these prior needs, if it asked also for endowment of the Natural Bases.

I wanted equally to realize both these aims—to make the School perfect in its existing scope and, by enlarging its scope, to make it more completely scientific in every sense. The answer on my second aim came to me only after the end of my time as Director.

★

Before I come to that, a few other enlargements in the work of the School call for record. As the School grew in size and

85

reputation, people with ideas came to look on it as good ground in which to plant their ideas and to water the ideas with money.

Thus, in the session 1928-9, a body known as the Commonwealth Fund gave to the School £400 a year to establish a course for welfare work in dealing with backward children, and followed this three years later by a much larger grant— £3,300 a year—for a course in Mental Health, which in 1934 was renewed for another three years.

The same year, 1928-9, that saw the beginning of Commonwealth Fund grant for Mental Health witnessed also interest of the Empire Marketing Board in promoting study at the School of 'Imperial Economic Problems', with a grant of £2,000 a year for five years, used in part to establish a Chair of Imperial Economic Relations. For whatever reason, this grant was not renewed after the original five years.

In the next session, 1929-30, a Committee representative of many important business firms offered to the School £5,000 a year for five years to establish a Department of Business Administration Research and Training, with the double aim of research into problems of business administration and of giving specialized training to selected students sent by the firms concerned. The offer was accepted and the Department got to work.

Near the end of the period covered in this book, in the session 1934-5, came another important enlargement in the teaching of the School. The course for the Commerce Degree had always included Modern Languages, but the teaching had been given at King's College. In this session, the teaching of all the main languages included was transferred to the School and a Modern Languages Department was established there, under a University Reader with a staff of seven full-time teachers and a substantial body of part-time assistants. This development came from within the School rather than from outside. Janet had always urged that understanding of a living language or languages other than one's own was an important essential to students of social science, too important to be farmed out to some other institution not concerned with social science. After much persuasion she carried conviction at last. Establishment of the Modern Languages Department was one of her great services to the School—nearly the last of them.[1]

A year later, in 1935-6, came one more new thing—a Civil Service Course designed to prepare students for entry by examination to that service. This course scored a resounding success in its first year. I have no doubt that it also was a suggestion of Janet's. She knew all about entry to the Civil Service.

At this point it is appropriate to return to the story of the Natural Bases of Social Science, broken off above in 1925. In June of that year I put the tangled problem of needs and priorities arising from my talks with Beardsley Ruml to the Emergency Committee in a memorandum. The Committee was our effective governing body, and since February 1925 had included two representatives of the Professorial Council, increased to three in 1928. The Committee told me to put both prior needs and Natural Bases of Social Science to Beardsley Ruml and I did so in the middle of July.

I prepared, in fact, two different letters covering different Memoranda, on July 15th and July 16th respectively. In the Memorandum of July 15th I put the prior needs first and proceeded to the Natural Bases of Social Science only at the end. But I did not send this Memorandum. Thinking over the emphasis which Ruml had laid on our developing the Natural Bases of Social Science, I reversed the order on July 16th. In the covering letter, I said to Ruml that I had put the Natural Bases first in the Memorandum, as he had suggested, but that 'actually the prior needs are by unfortunate necessity really prior'.

Here is the plan for making the circle of the Social Sciences complete which, as instructed by our Emergency Committee,

---

[1] The last significant action of Janet in the School, taken after my departure in 1937, related to this Modern Languages Department. Lord Sankey, one of the L.S.E. Governors, came to see her a month or two before her own retirement at the end of September 1938, and asked if there was anything particularly near her heart that he could do for her before she went. He was one of the Sir Ernest Cassel Trustees who had endowed so many teaching posts for the Commerce Degree. They had, she knew, £20,000 still unappropriated. She asked him, if he could, to persuade his fellow Trustees to endow at the School the salary of the head of the Modern Languages Department—not by the language he professed but in virtue of his position. Lord Sankey agreed and it was done.

I prepared and sent to Beardsley Ruml on July 16, 1925 and which I have found again in my papers today, thirty-four years after, in making final revision of this book for the press.

THE NATURAL BASES OF THE SOCIAL SCIENCES

'The existing departments of the London School of Economics and Political Science fall into two main groups, corresponding roughly to the two parts of its title. One group is concerned with economic relations of men and comprises, beside the department of Economics in the narrow sense, such subjects as accounting and business organisation, banking and currency, commerce and industry, and transport. In the other group, concerned with political and social relations, are politics and public administration, international relations, sociology, and law. History and statistics are common to both groups.

'To complete the circle of the social sciences, a third group of studies is required, dealing with the natural bases of economics and politics, with the human material and with its physical environment, and forming a bridge between the natural and the social sciences. On the side of human material there should be included here such subjects as Anthropology, 'Social Biology' (genetics, population, vital statistics, heredity, eugenics and dysgenics), Physiology so far as it bears on problems of fatigue and nutrition, Economic Psychology, and Public Health. On the side of physical environment come Geography in its widest sense as a study of natural resources, Agriculture and Meteorology. This third group already receives some attention at the School of Economics. Its full development—the addition of the missing third to the existing structure of the School—would be perhaps the most important step that could be taken now for the development of the social sciences. Apart from its direct value in advancing the borders of human knowledge, it would confer a great indirect benefit by bringing the natural and social sciences into contact and importing the methods of the former into the latter.

'In practice it would mean adding to the School at least four new professorships with adequate departmental resources of junior staff and accommodation, for

Anthropology
Social Biology
Economic Psychology
Public Health

and strengthening the existing department of Geography on its physical side.

'In Anthropology there is now at the School a small (less than half-time) Chair of Ethnology and a Readership in Social Anthropology. A full-time Chair of Anthropology with sufficient junior staff to allow for ample travel and field work is needed.

'In Social Biology there is no post. Special courses of lectures on problems of heredity have been given in recent years with marked success and meet an obvious demand. In this field it is not desired, of course, to establish a biological laboratory. What is wanted is to get a man of biological training to learn economics and politics and then and only then apply himself to economic and social problems. Actual investigation would be mainly statistical.

'In Economic Psychology a beginning has been made in co-operation with the National Institute of Industrial Psychology, whose Director is a member of the School staff. It is understood that an application for assistance is being made to the Trustees by the Institute and it is hoped that this application may be considered favourably. For the development of Economic Psychology, however, as a subject of University study and teaching, in conjunction with the other social sciences, an important teaching post and other expenditure are indispensable at the School of Economics as well.

'In Public Health there is equally room and need for a border line study, stretching out from a medical basis into such subjects as town planning, housing, or vital statistics. No provision is yet made for this.

'The holders of these chairs if they were established would naturally often work on converging lines. Full investigation, for instance, of the problem of "deficiency" (whether manifested in crime or pauperism or disease or lunacy) would call for contributions from all four as well as from specialists in other branches of the School's work, such as law and economics. No one person could combine in himself all the previous experience necessary: that is the reason for suggesting four separate chairs . . .

'Complete endowment from the beginning, however, of the whole development is neither necessary nor desirable. In some cases it would be necessary to offer permanence to get the right man, but in others the post should be frankly experimental. In some cases also the establishment of any teaching post ought to depend upon knowing that a person of the right qualifications was available to fill it. Permanent provision sufficient for perhaps two out of the four posts suggested above, together with a renewable grant for a period of years, would meet the position financially. To this should be added a grant in aid of building without which any new development is impossible; a definite scheme of extension of building in Houghton Street is described below.

'The School authorities are deeply interested in developing the social sciences in the manner indicated. They have already made a beginning in most of the fields of study affected and they will take further steps from time to time as they are able. But the pressure on the School's finances for work within its existing spheres rules out the possibility of any large development with its general funds. It must first provide for certain prior needs.'

There followed on this an even longer statement of our urgent prior needs.

In reply came an interim friendly letter from Ruml thanking me and the Secretary of the School for all that we had done to make his time in London interesting. Then he got to work with his Trustees, and as soon as I could escape from the Royal Commission on Coal Mines which absorbed me from September 1925 to March 1926, and was followed by the Vice-Chancellorship of London University in June 1926, I proceeded to discussion with teachers and with the Professorial Council as a whole.

One of my first steps, in May 1926, was to discuss with a meeting of the teachers in the various departments appearing to be concerned, possible developments of School work that might follow on grants by the Laura Spelman Rockefeller Memorial. After a meeting with eight such teachers, I was left to explore the matter further with individuals and groups concerned and to bring forward proposals for another meeting.

There resulted, at a further meeting of teachers held on November 26th, a Report covering three foolscap pages, dealing not only with the Natural Bases of Social Science in general, but discussing many separate branches, such as Social Anthropology, Social Biology, Social Psychology, Public Health and Criminology. The Report ended by pointing out also the important borderland between the School's work and sciences concerned with man's physical environment, from Geography to Geology, Botany and Meteorology.

On December 1, 1926, this Report, in favour of going ahead on the Natural Bases of Social Science, came for discussion to a meeting of the Professorial Council attended by twenty-eight teaching members, and found universal support. A few minor amendments were made, chiefly to avoid any suggestion that the teaching of Sociology at the School had failed in the past. With these amendments, acceptance of the Report was proposed by Professor Hobhouse and Professor Wolf, and carried unanimously by the Professorial Council.

With this resolution of the Professorial Council in my pocket, I dashed off to America in the Christmas week of 1926 and achieved four distinct objects.

I asked and obtained from the Laura Spelman Rockefeller Memorial $500,000 for the Natural Bases and International Relations and $175,000 for prior needs.

I discussed the Bloomsbury Site with Raymond Fosdick of the Rockefeller Foundation and received from John D. Rockefeller the Second a promise of $50,000 to buy an option on the Site—ample guarantee of larger help from the Foundation when the London Senate was ready to ask for it.

I secured Allyn Young from Harvard as our first full-time Professor of Political Economy.

I arranged, through Samuel Insull, for Philip Mair to get the chance he wanted, of starting life in Pekin, Illinois, on development of electricity. I started home with all my sheaves on January 14, 1927.

Nearly all the prior needs and most of our other desires were met in practice at once. Allyn Young came over from Harvard but fell ill and died in 1929; this was a great misfortune, for he was just the man to make economics as the Founders and I wished it to be. Chairs of Anthropology and International Law were established at once, to be filled by Bronislaw Malinowski and Arnold McNair. *New Survey of London Life and Labour,* mentioned already in Chapter IV, began at once.

Our most daring adventure of all, the Chair and Department of Social Biology, took longer to start. We had to wait till accommodation could be built in Houghton Street, where the houses acquired by compulsion had just been placed at our disposal. We had to find a Professor of Social Biology. All that we could do at once was to offer two research studentships in that new subject. And in the end our adventure did not last.

We waited till, in January 1930, we had found one who seemed to be the ideal first Professor of Social Biology in Lancelot Hogben. He was chosen, from a largish field of candidates, unanimously, by a Board of Advisers on which the School was represented by Sidney Webb, Arthur Bowley, Harold Laski and myself. Contrary to our first idea, we gave him what seemed ample accommodation, including a small laboratory. His Department produced in 1935 a Report on its first five years of work, with a formidable list of scientific papers issued by it. But, for whatever reason, he did not find himself happy with us.

He was valued highly by natural scientists and was made a Fellow of the Royal Society at 40, in 1936. Long before the end of that year, other posts were being offered to him and he was being pressed particularly to go to Aberdeen. I made an attempt to keep him, describing him to Josiah Stamp, our Chairman of Governors, as 'certainly the most distinguished member of our staff and a brilliant mind which it would be a disaster to lose'.

My efforts proved vain. Early in 1937 Hogben decided to accept the Regius Chair of Natural History at Aberdeen and offered his resignation to us.

Four of the Professorial Council who had joined ten years before in the unanimous resolution of welcome to Social Biology proposed now that the Chair should be suspended. I wondered at the time whether they would have proposed this, if Professor Hobhouse had been alive. He had moved the resolution of welcome and his field was in some ways nearer to Social Biology than that of any other teacher. But Hobhouse had died in 1929.

The Emergency Committee decided in March 1937 that the future of Social Biology must be regarded as an open question. They could hardly do otherwise. A month before I had accepted an invitation to become Master of University College, Oxford. The issue raised by Hogben's resignation was one for a new Director to consider. On February 10, 1938, the Governors decided against continuing the Chair of Social Biology.

I felt disappointed at this decision, as I did at the change of attitude of teachers who had supported Social Biology before and now came out against it. Both as a schoolboy at Charterhouse and as an undergraduate at Oxford I had been kept mainly to Latin and Greek, with mathematics as a side-show and with Hebrew thrown in for my last year at school. But my free bent, in serious reading, had been towards natural science always. I had meant once to be an astronomer and when I gave that up, I clung all the more eagerly to biology. At Charterhouse, when we won prizes, we were allowed within reasonable limits to choose our own books. My first prize, by free choice, was Wallace on *Natural Selection* followed by Darwin's *Origin of Species*. Before I ended school, I had got on to *Man's Place in Nature* by T. H. Huxley, and at Oxford, where still I was a classic mainly, I became one of Huxley's devotees; four volumes of his lectures and essays, reaching out from natural science to social problems, all bought in my Oxford time between 1899 and 1902, stand on my shelves today. My first address in character as Director of the School, in October 1920, on 'Economics as a Liberal Education' centred round Huxley's address of 1854 leading to his appeal for a Science of Society. One of the many unexpected pleasures that writing this book has brought me, is realizing once more that University College, Oxford—my own college as Fellow and Master—once invited Huxley to be its Master.

But my dear old School of Economics, after I had spent more years there than at Charterhouse and at Oxford together, would have nothing of my Science of Society as learned from Huxley and other men of science.

I wish still that the great adventure on which Janet and Beardsley Ruml and I embarked in 1925 and to which, a year later, we persuaded the whole Professorial Council, had led to a permanent result. The result would have been good for economics, as economics was understood by the Founders of the School.

For Sidney and Beatrice, as for myself, economics was not an analysis of concepts but an inference from facts of society after unsparing examination. It seemed to me then, as it seems still, irrational to study society without studying the human material from which society is made. Society has a natural basis in men and women, and cannot be understood by people who insist on being ignorant of the basis. I may be allowed to add that the happy contacts which I have enjoyed since 1933 with men of natural science, in seeking to save learning from Hitler, Mussolini and their fellow-tyrants, make me regret even more anything that keeps natural science and social science apart.

METHOD OF SOCIAL SCIENCE

But, by the time that I left the School, economic and political studies in Britain were still far from being conducted by the methods of the natural sciences, as our Founders had desired.

As has been told in an earlier chapter, it fell to me on June 24, 1937, to make as my farewell to the School the customary Oration in Commemoration Week. I took as my subject *The Place of the Social Sciences in Human Knowledge*.[1] I illustrated my view of economics as we still had it in 1937, not by anything in the School of Economics, but by reference to a book published a year before by the best-known British economist of that day—Maynard Keynes—on *The General Theory of Employment Interest and Money*, and to the reviews which other economists had given to it.

I contrasted Keynes' book with the methods by which Einstein had revolutionized our understanding of one part of physical nature. 'Einstein started from facts—the Morley Mitcheson measurements of light, the movements of the planet Mercury, the unexplained aberrancies of the moon

[1] Published in *Politica* of September 1937.

from its predicted place'—'Einstein went back to facts or told others where they should go, to confirm or to reject his theory . . . ' 'Mr. Keynes starts, not from any fact, but from the definition of a concept, of what he (Mr. Keynes) means when he says "involuntary unemployment" . . . Mr. Keynes does not return to facts for verification. There is no page throughout his work on which a generalization is set against marshalled facts for testing.'

I turned to the reviewers—three acknowledged leaders among professional economists. Not one of them, I declared, suggested that Keynes' theory should be tested by facts or asked how it compared with facts. 'The distinguishing mark of economic science, as illustrated by this debate, is that it is a science in which verification of generalizations by reference to facts is neglected as irrelevant.' I went on to a famous profession of faith by William Harvey: 'I profess to learn and to teach anatomy, not from books, but from dissections; not from the positions of philosophers, but from the fabric of nature.' In contrast to this, a large part of economic writing today was 'argument from the positions of philosophers—of Ricardo, or Karl Marx or Marshall, or the Austrian School or the Stockholm School' and so on.

These criticisms, it is needless to point out, were not directed against anything in the School itself. As has been shown in Chapter IV of this book, the School in my period of review had produced a mass of factual studies of human society and its organization growing steadily from year to year. It had failed only in converting sufficiently to the new gospel of Sidney and Beatrice the heathen in Cambridge and other outlying places, who still clung to theory untested by facts.

The London School of Economics and Political Science, even after forty-two years, had not achieved the purposes for which Sidney and Beatrice Webb had brought it to birth—the purpose of breaking up economics and making it a science in the true sense of that word, and the purpose of making the circle of the Social Sciences complete. But the School, with the never-failing help of its Founders, had become a rather wonderful place.

I ceased to be Director of the School of Economics on

September 30, 1937; Janet ceased to be Secretary of the School just a year after. In saying farewell to Janet, in his first annual Report on the Work of the School, the new Director emphasized her devoted service to the students and her friendship for them. In paying tribute to me in June 1937, Sidney Webb described what happened in my eighteen years as a re-foundation. He began by emphasizing, as a new thing in the School, the creation there in those years of a University atmosphere, between student and teacher, between one student and another, between one teacher and another. He ended by expressing a hope:

'It may be that, when the end comes, he will look back on the Second Foundation of the London School of Economics between 1919-37, as one of the greatest and most valuable achievements of his crowded life.'

In answer to that hope, today, in the Webb Centenary year, I can say only that I look back, as Janet looked back, on our years at the School together as being years as happy, busy and exciting as either of us ever experienced. In so far as the School made progress in those years, it did so by learning something from older institutions and becoming in some ways more like them, while remaining different in other ways.

The School of Economics, between 1919 and 1937, while retaining its evening students, acquired for the first time a large student body similar to that of older Universities—young men and young women preparing for work, not already at work. It applied to this student body a lesson learned in older Universities, of the need for personal contact and friendship throughout University life between teacher and student, and between one student and another. It treasured and encouraged both love of learning and the light-heartedness of youth.

With this assimilation to older Universities, the School of Economics retained three special advantages over most of them;

First, the School brought young students preparing for life into contact with a substantial body of older people who, though working already, were students still and set the example of learning throughout life.

Second, the School brought British students into contact with overseas students to an extent unparalleled elsewhere.

11 *The main Library*

12   *Roof of the new Houghton Street building, with Graham Wallas Room above*

Third, the School's range of studies, in novelty and in its proved attractive power on eager minds, was not surpassed elsewhere.

That the School of Economics could become like this it owed to two characteristics of one man: first, to Sidney Webb's genius in divining seventy years ago just what kind of new University institution, with what range of studies, was most needed in the world; second, to Sidney Webb's unselfishness and lack of vanity. To one Director of the School after another Sidney left freedom to take his own line and at the same time stood ready to give at any moment just what help and counsel was needed. The secret of achievement is not power but co-operation.

I was delighted to be asked to deliver on July 14, 1959, a Centenary Lecture on Sidney Webb and the London School of Economics. I am happier still to be able to print the substance of what I said then, and much more also about Sidney and Beatrice, in the closing chapter of this book about their School.

IX

CENTENARY OF THE WEBBS

THE WEBB ACHIEVEMENT

SIDNEY WEBB was born on July 14, 1859, and died on October 13, 1947. Beatrice Potter, who became Mrs. Sidney Webb, was born on January 22, 1858, and died on April 30, 1943. But they decided very sensibly to have been born officially on the same day and celebrated their seventieth birthday together in 1929, when their portrait was put up in the Founders' Room of the School of Economics. For me 1959 is the Centenary Year of Sidney and Beatrice Webb alike.

To my mind they are among the dozen most important people of the past hundred years. I say this although I did not share their political opinions at any time; I shared their political opinions even less than before, when they passed from being Socialist to being Communist. But I was a friend of theirs for forty years, to the very end of their lives; I saw them at work for all those years; I had the delight of working with them often, above all for eighteen years in the London School of Economics and Political Science. That I believe is the greatest single contribution made to humanity by the Webbs and naturally in this lecture I give more time to it than to any other work of theirs. But it is one contribution only out of many that they made to humanity. The thing above all that should be emphasized about the Webbs in their Centenary Year is the breadth and quality and variety of their achievement.

They are the inventors of the idea of a national minimum standard of life, to be guaranteed and enforced by the State, while leaving freedom and responsibility for the individual to manage his own affairs above that minimum. This idea, laid down by the Webbs in 1903, is the germ of the Beveridge Report of 1942. The fact that the Webbs did not like compulsory social insurance as a means of finding the necessary funds for the national minimum represents a difference of method rather than of principle. The fact that social insurance does not today provide enough to provide the necessary minimum, but has to be eked out by assistance under means test represents a more serious defect of social policy by inflation. I have to return to this problem of inflation before I end.

The Webbs, again, are the authors of many volumes of highly original writing on social and political institutions, from the History of Trade Unionism which was their first joint task, through eighteen volumes on Local Government, Poor Law History, and Poor Law problems, to arguments for Socialism or Communism. I once estimated their total book output at 5,000,000 words, well over 10,000 pages of a sustained high quality.

The national minimum and these books, added to the School of Economics, are three services to humanity sufficient in themselves to justify the rank among our greatest people that I have assigned to the Webbs. But these three services are as far as possible from completing the picture of their achievement.

One must think in addition to the contributions of the Webbs to School Education, above all in London; of the University of London Constitution of 1900 invented with Haldane; of the 'Charlottenburg Scheme' for the Imperial College of Science and Technology, also invented with Haldane and realized in 1907; of the Royal Commission on Poor Law from 1905 to 1909 and the resulting organization established in 1909 for the Break-up of the Poor Law; of the *New Statesman* in 1913; of the course that they set for the Labour Party in 1918, by *Labour and the New Social Order*; of all that Sidney did as Minister of the Crown; and of the parties at Passfield Corner. As I put it in a sentence once,[1] 'It is not easy for any honest writer on the last sixty years to get away from the Webbs.'

If one asks, as one can hardly help asking, what made this unexampled achievement possible, the answer falls into two stages. The achievement was due, first and foremost, to the

[1] *Power and Influence*, p. 25.

Personal Qualities of Sidney and Beatrice; I have set these out shortly in my next section. But there were Contributory Factors also. One such factor was the period in which their lives fell—from 1858 to the early 1940's. A second factor was the extent to which they were able to use and did use other people to carry out their plans; this, I believe, has an interesting explanation in one of their personal qualities—that of openness to new ideas—but is best discussed separately.

PERSONAL QUALITIES AND OTHER FACTORS

What were the personal qualities which made possible the achievement of the Webbs, spread over so many different fields?

First, of course, among Webb qualities, was the sheer intellectual power of each of them, differing but fitting into one another. I have given more than one example of how the two together reached a better conclusion than either might have done alone.

There was, second, their complete independence of view and fearlessness in expressing views. Let me take one example arising out of Beatrice's appreciation of how much she owed to financial ease. During a period of illness which descended on her in 1916, she made a remark on health service that is highly apposite today:

'One of the highest privileges of the well-to-do is to be able to live in comfort and perfect health conditions when they are ill. Shall we have the wit to communalize this advantage? It would mean not only the necessary national expenditure, but also all sorts of precautions against malingering. How do I know that I am not malingering?'[1]

Have we by 1959 had the wit, in our National Health Service, to escape the danger which Beatrice foresaw in 1916? The Beatrice Webb Diaries abound in suggestive questions and comments like this, as do Beatrice's two other books—*My Apprenticeship* and *Our Partnership*.

There was, third, their freedom both from rancour and from creator's vanity,[1] or as I put it in another place, in speaking of Sidney, his unselfishness. One illustration which I gave

[1] *Diaries*, 1912-24, p. xv.

of this unselfishness was the way in which, to avoid a quarrel
with the railway companies who were objecting to something
that he had said about railway-men's wages, he resigned the
Chairmanship of Governors of the School. 'But it remained
true of the Governors, as of many other gatherings that where-
ever Sidney Webb happened to sit, there was the Chair—the
source of ideas and practical expedients and reconciling
compromises.'[1]

There was, fourth, their concentration. Walking round
Beachy Head with Beatrice one day, after she and I had
amused ourselves by laughing over Wells' *New Machiavelli*,
I happened to ask her about some common friends of ours—
had she seen them recently? 'No,' she answered, 'I see nothing
now of the T's. There is nothing at which we are working in
common and I cannot afford the time for purely social inter-
course.' I was young and felt that at the time to be a little
inhuman, but a passage following soon after in the Diaries
gives a completely disarming defence. 'It is remarkable how
limited one's circle becomes when one is at once elderly and
hardworking.'[2]

It was part of the Webb concentration that they never, to
my knowledge, played games of any kind. And when I asked
Beatrice once about plays on the stage, she told me that she
never went to see any plays except those of Bernard Shaw,
and then only because he was a friend.[3]

There was, fifth, their passion for new ideas. This is the
most important of all their qualities—so important that I
leave it for discussion later.

In any account of personal qualities, one more feature must
be included—Beatrice's gift for walking. Whether or not it
contributed to the Webb's achievements, it was remarkable
in itself. As I put it in some memories written just after her
death, Beatrice was a great walker and to walk with her was
to exercise body and mind together.

'She was a living refutation of Hugh Sidgwick's dictum in
'Walking Essays' that it is possible either to walk and babble,

[1] *The Webbs and Their Work*, pp. 51-2.
[2] *Diaries, 1912-24*, p. 14. July 12, 1913.
[3] *Power and Influence*, p. 63.

or to talk and amble, but not to walk and talk at the same time.[1]

★

The achievement of Sidney and Beatrice was due above all to their personal qualities. But they themselves would have been the first to admit that they owed something also to good luck.

Beatrice, through her father, had an assured income of £1,000 a year. She said often how much the work that Sidney and she did depended on this income and the freedom that it gave them from financial cares. That was a piece of good luck not only for them but for us who have gained so much through their work.

But they enjoyed ease of mind in another way also which many people miss today. They were never without excellent domestic service, and had no need to stop writing books in order to make beds or wash dishes. In the record of happiness which Beatrice wrote in July 1921, she names as one factor in her happiness and Sidney's that their servants were devoted to them.

In the light of these two freedoms, from financial anxiety and from domestic tasks, it seems fair to attribute to Sidney and Beatrice one other piece of good luck, in the years of their living and dying. They had the best of the nineteenth century for people with fixed incomes. They died before the inflation of 1939 had got under way; if they had been born and died thirty years later their £1,000 a year would have been worth £300 a year to them. They had the best of the nineteenth century for comfort and ease at home; they died before domestic service became rarer than diamonds.

It is a chastening thought to realize that if two people, with the abilities of Sidney and Beatrice and their £1,000 a year but born thirty years later, had set out to render exactly the same service to humanity, they might have found this impossible because they lacked freedom from financial anxiety and domestic tasks. Curmudgeons of my age must be forgiven if, every now and again, we wonder what the society of the future will be like, if the spiritual successors of Sidney and Beatrice have to make their own beds and wash their own dishes, while so many people with more leisure than the Victorians dreamed

[1] *The Highway*, November 1945.

of may be using their leisure to no good purpose.

Another contributory factor to the total achievement of the Webbs was their use of others to carry on what they had started.

As soon as the Ministry Report of the Poor Law Commission had been produced, Beatrice, with her co-signatory Russell Wakefield, and Sidney as Chairman of its Executive Committee, set up organization for pushing over the Report. This was in May 1909. A year later, in May 1910, she was asking herself: 'Can we give this organization an existence independent of our leadership—exactly as we have done in the case of the London School of Economics?'[1]

This question contains in itself another secret of Webb achievement. Sidney and Beatrice were never content to be thinking about one thing only at a time. Once they had started anything, they looked for someone else to carry it on, and they succeeded generally in their search. They were good judges as a rule of people, they were persuasive in their invitations, and it was known that they could be trusted to help at need the successor who took their job on.

If the question is asked why they always looked for a successor, the answer, to my mind, lies in what I have named as the fifth of their personal qualities: 'passion for new ideas'. This meant that they were always wanting to try something new, whether it was labour exchanges as in 1905, or Soviet Communism nearly thirty years later. And they were able to try something new, whenever a happy thought came to them, largely because of the first contributory factor—the safe £1,000 a year. They never had to take a job or stick to a job because of the money it brought.

MY CONTACTS WITH THE WEBBS

I must have met the Webbs first at about the same time as I became an occasional student of the School of Economics, attending in 1904 or 1905 lectures by A. L. Bowley on Statistics and by H. S. Foxwell. But, so far as I know, contact with the Founders of the School was not due in any way to the School itself. It arose through their and my interest in the same social problems. I believe that I talked to them for the

[1] *Our Partnership*, p. 453.

first time late in 1904, seeking to persuade them of my pet hobby, labour exchanges, as a necessary part of the cure for unemployment. As from 1905 onwards, I was immersed in dealing with unemployment by day (on the Central Unemployed Body for London) and writing about it and other social problems by night (on the *Morning Post*), while they were immersed in the Royal Commission on Poor Law and the Relief of Distress through Unemployment. Consultation and co-operation became continuous between us. They helped me in every possible way.

As these activities led them to the making of the Minority Report of the Commission in 1909 and starting in 1910 an organization to push the Report and break up the Poor Law, while it led me to become a Civil Servant, directing labour exchanges and organizing unemployment insurance, we saw for a time much less of one another. So far as I know, the only letter that passed between us in any of the years 1910 to 1912 was a letter of thanks from Beatrice for my second book, *John and Irene : An Anthology of Thoughts on Women* that I had given to her.

And in World War I, while I was engaged in one war activity after another, either Munition Making or Food Control, they concerned themselves largely with problems of Reconstruction. Beatrice became a member of the Government Reconstruction Committee in February 1917 and rejoiced, by the end of that year, in having piloted the Minority Report proposals through its Local Government Committee, with the help of Lord George Hamilton. Of course, they were doing many other things also at the same time—on the Fabian Research Department, and, in framing Labour policy for the future. 'Sidney,' wrote Beatrice in December 1917, 'has become the intellectual leader of the Labour Party.'[1]

Letters between us had begun again in 1913 through Sidney inviting my subscription to the *New Statesman*. Thereafter consultation was resumed on unemployment, pensions, and other problems. 'I wish you were on this Committee,' said Beatrice to me in inviting me to a quiet evening of talk on

[1] *Diaries, 1912-24,* p. 99.

'demobilization, etc.', just after she had been put on the Reconstruction Committee.

Then, out of the blue in May 1919, came Sidney's invitation to me to become the fourth nurse to his favourite child, the London School of Economics. This proceeding is typical Sidney. While the School had been running happily under Hewins and Mackinder in peace, he had come in occasionally only. When the prospective return of peace seemed to call for large measures, including a new full-time Director, more space and money for building, and more money for teaching, he not only chose the Director, but took all the essential steps about money and building. This has been told in Chapter I and calls for no repetition here. But other instances will be given in a moment of his and Beatrice's parental attitude to their School.

I have treated Sidney and Beatrice as inseparable for the purpose of this chapter, as I did in the centenary lecture from which the chapter sprang. They are inseparable, because having come together they pursued, always together, an overwhelming common purpose, of making and spreading ideas on social organization. They would each have done splendid work in this field separately: Sidney did such work in the Fabian Society before they had met; Beatrice did it in the chapters on Dock Labour which she wrote for Charles Booth, when she had just broken with Joseph Chamberlain, and which I still remember reading with admiration when I began to study unemployment in Whitechapel nearly sixty years ago. But, of course, they did far better work together, just because they were not identical. They were complementary, as a right and a left hand are complementary—not the same.

Some day, before too long I hope, the similarities and differences between them will be set out, with full use of all the relevant documents, many of which still await publication. I cannot do more than give a few impressions.

To begin with, Beatrice was more purely bookish than Sidney. She did not learn through conversation with others as he did. I have given elsewhere an example of my personal experience of this.[1] She was more bookish also in the sense

[1] *Power and Influence*, p. 62.

that, of the two elements in their common purpose of making and spreading ideas, she was far more interested in the making and was apt to regard the spreading as a rather tiresome consequence—something to hand to others, like washing up after a meal.

Beatrice's handwriting, after her marriage at least, was nearly or quite illegible, while Sidney's was as clear as print. From examination of a honeymoon letter which was printed in *An Epic of Clare Market* [1] and to which both Sidney and Beatrice contributed, Janet suggests that Beatrice may have been easier to read before marriage than after it, when she had Sidney's copper-plate always at her command, so that readability came to matter less.

Sidney did a great deal more talking to others and persuading them. He became a politician, as I do not think Beatrice ever wished to be. And Sidney put in far more time at the School of Economics than Beatrice did. The School was his favourite child rather than hers.

This leads me to a possible difference of view between them, which I put only with some hesitation. Sidney realized that, if the School was to serve a good purpose, it must be impartial, allowing complete freedom of teaching and research to every individual who worked there. It may not be without significance that when Bernard Shaw, having regard to the Hutchinson bequest, was objecting to impartiality for the School, he wrote, not to Sidney, but to Beatrice.[2] In 1933, at any rate when Soviet Communism was on the stocks, Beatrice wrote to me about a book [3] she had been reading which raised in her mind the question 'whether or not the study of institutions can be scientific in the sense of being quite impartial—as impartial as the study of flora and fauna'. I fear that she might not have been as sound as Sidney, on absolute impartiality for the School.

SIDNEY'S FAVOURITE CHILD

I have called the London School of Economics and Political Science in the University of London by Beatrice's pet name

---

[1] pp. 9-10.
[2] *Epic of Clare Market*, pp. 27-8.
[3] *Towards the Understanding of Karl Marx* by Sidney Hook.

for it. This does not mean that Beatrice herself did nothing there. She was often extremely active, and held strong views both as to the methods it should adopt and as to its scope.

When the School was only just born, though it had an excellent nurse in the Director Hewins, it kept the parents also very busy. There was one occasion, for instance, in October 1896 when the School was being moved from its first home in John Street to a new home in Adelphi Terrace and Hewins worried himself into an illness and had to be sent off for a rest. Each day Sidney trudged over to the Adelphi directly after breakfast to spend 'his mornings with painters, plumbers and locksmiths, interviewing would-be students to whom he gives fatherly advice'. Beatrice arranged details of housekeeping for the School, while getting on slowly with her book. 'Obvious that this institution will take up much of our time for the next few years'.[1]

On the same page, *Our Partnership* records another long day spent at the School in the search for a political science lecturer from among candidates who had applied in answer to an advertisement. The search failed utterly. Sidney was looking for someone to lecture on different systems of municipal taxation, while the candidates offered him lectures on Utopias from More downwards, or 'Political Man' or 'Land under the Tudors'. 'Finally,' says Beatrice, 'we determined to do without our lecturer—to my mind a blessed consummation. It struck me always as a trifle difficult to teach a science which does not yet exist.'

These birth pains for the School passed almost at once: Nurse Hewins took charge, and Sidney and Beatrice found plenty of time for other things. By 1902, when Sidney was getting into trouble with most of his left wing friends for supporting the Conservative Education Bill, Beatrice described Hewins, Sidney and herself as an excellent working trio, Hewins in charge of the whole internal organization, with Sidney responsible for finance, with her own job that of roping in influential supporters from among old friends and connections.

Apart from his lectures and occasional addresses, Sidney

---

[1] *Our Partnership*, p. 94.

and Beatrice's job, by Mackinder's time, became largely a social one, of bringing staff and students and distinguished outsiders together by dinners or parties. And with the Poor Law Commission and the campaign for breaking up of the Poor Law they became absorbed in a fresh burst of new ideas.

The growing of the School out of the thoughts of one of its parents cannot be illustrated better than by comparing references to the School in each of three books by Beatrice: *Our Partnership* running from 1892 to 1911, her *Diaries 1912-1924*, and her *Diaries 1924-1932*. All three books are diaries in effect, recording experiences and impressions of particular days, though with varying degrees of revision or working up later.

Our Partnership is full of references to the School directly, as well as to other matters like the University of London, affecting the interests of the School.

In the *Diaries 1912-1924* the School of Economics practically does not appear except as an example of something going its own way successfully, with a life of its own. If only the *New Statesman* and the Fabian Research would do the same, cries Beatrice, so that I could 'retire into a life of research and social companionship' (February 14, 1915).

The School appears again in this set of Diaries only after I was at work, with Sidney in November 1919 helping me to organize the new developments at the School and 'acting very much as if he was Chairman'. But it is significant that the same diary entry tells also that Beatrice for the last six weeks had helped Sidney on the three final chapters of the *History of Trade Unionism,* involving research into the genesis of new ideas. Sidney and Beatrice were never content to do one thing only at a time.

In the *Diaries 1924-1932* the School of Economics has no place even in the index. Sidney and Beatrice in relation to the School are noticed chiefly as having their portrait painted for the Founders' Room. Beatrice found this process rather tiresome, but came round in the end to welcome the beauty of the room, and what I said of them there as 'a very faithful admirer'.

The School never grew out of Sidney's thoughts to anything like the same extent. He proved himself the ideal father to a healthy child—leaving the child to run by itself as soon as it could, coming in to give help at all critical times, finding throughout his life reasons for having a look at the child and showing his love.

One critical time arose in the very early days when Ramsay MacDonald—a chronic enemy of the Webbs—seized the chance of Sidney and Beatrice's absence in America to try to strangle their child by cutting down the Technical Education Board grant.[1]

A call for father came whenever a new Director had to be found. Sidney, in fact, chose all the Directors up to and including myself; that he should have the choice of me was the more notable because he had ceased for a good many years to be the Chairman of the Governors, while the actual Chairman was an old Balliol friend of mine. Sidney's choice of Directors made more plain than anything else that he put the School above party. The steps that he took at the time of my appointment to give the School the best possible start after World War I have been described above.

Finally, Sidney was always in love with his child. I have a moving letter of his, from the Colonial Office in 1931, saying that he wishes not to drop out of touch with the School, and expressing his longing to be free from office as Minister. He went on making one occasion after another for coming to the School and bringing others there. I welcomed him, of course, in every way.

Nor was his love for the School affected by its having failed to grow up just as he and Beatrice had planned. They had hoped to 'break up economics', replacing analysis of concepts by collection and examination of facts, and, as has been shown above, they did not want theoretical politics either. They had hoped for contact between natural science and social science, with biology and mathematics as introductions to an economics degree. They had enjoyed a moment of apparent success for this second aim with the establishment of Social Biology. I have a letter from Beatrice in 1933, while Hogben was with us, rejoicing over the widening that I had achieved in widening the scope of social science. This widening did not last.

[1] See *Epic of Clare Market*, pp. 41-4.

But Sidney was a fond enough father to go on loving his child however it grew up.

PASSION FOR NEW IDEAS

I have named, as the most important of all the qualities of Sidney and Beatrice, their passion for new ideas. It explains many things that they did.

It explains, in the first place, their readiness, and indeed eagerness, to hand over their ideas to others for carrying on. It is sufficient to give one example of many that could be given from Beatrice's own words. The Majority and Minority Reports of the Poor Law Commission were signed in January 1909. In May 1909 the National Committee for the Break-up of the Poor Law—an organization for putting over the Minority Report—was launched. In May 1910 Beatrice asks: 'Can we give this organization an existence independent of our leadership—exactly as we have done with the London School of Economics?'[1] She is wanting to get back to research, and cannot do so, if she has to spend energy of her own on propaganda. In May 1914 one finds her regretting that the Fabian Research Department cannot be taken over like the School of Economics and looking forward hopefully to 'graceful retirement' from the New Statesman, once it is safe financially.[2]

It explains, in the second place, their readiness to take up new causes. Sidney and Beatrice were the first important people to accept my fetish of National Labour Exchanges. They fell for Soviet Communism, I believe, essentially because it seemed to them something new.

The first sign of interest in Russia that is recorded in Beatrice's diaries is on February 20, 1930, when she and Sidney entertained the Russian Ambassador Sokolnikov to dinner.[3] Thereafter interest becomes increasingly apparent in 1930 and in the political troubles of 1931. By January of 1932, Beatrice was contrasting the live creation of Soviet Russia, under the Communist Party, as a religious order, with the dead body of the Webb Constitution for a Socialist Commonwealth, and by April the pair had decided on a pilgrimage to Moscow, from

[1] *Our Partnership*, p. 453.
[2] *Diaries*, 1912-24, p. 24.
[3] *Diaries*, 1924-32, p. 236.

which they returned at the end of July, having travelled 5,000 miles over Russia 'from the Baltic to the Black Sea, and from near the Caspian to not far from the Polish frontier'.[1]

In the letter telling me of this journey, Sidney said he must now finish off the book on Methods of Social Study which he had sent to me in proof for criticisms. But clearly they must have got to work very fast indeed on Soviet Communism.

In September 1934, while Sidney was in Moscow again, Beatrice told me that ten out of twelve chapters had been finished and that Part 1 would go to the printer as soon as Sidney returned. By early October 1935 all was finished, the index was sent off, and 'Sidney is already considering how he can employ himself this next autumn, and how he can be useful to the School'.

There was much discussion of their theme between the Webbs and myself in the years from 1933 to 1936. I had given them lengthy comments on their Planning Chapter as early as January of 1934. The gist of these comments was that they had produced a very impressive picture which would be made still more impressive by open recognition:

'(a) that the statistics are those of the interested Government,
 (b) that it is far too early to say whether the spring of material progress and change supplied by capitalist enterprise in other countries, will be effectively replaced by anything else in Russia.'

A year later we came to outright difference on another issue. I confessed to having an open mind 'with a sneaking desire to see a planned economy fairly tested out' (presumably in some other country than Britain):

'But it does hurt me to think of any cause in which I could be interested or any persons for whom I care being associated with the kind of brutality represented by the present Russian regime or appearing in any way to condone or make light of it.'

I went on to give my evidence of this brutality, but I think that the evidence for my case was supplied by Beatrice herself, when a year or two later she sent me a Memorandum of what she thought about the Moscow trials of Radak and her former friend Sokolnikov. The gist of this was that Czarist repression

[1] S.W. to me July 20, 1932.

had made conspiracy, treachery and revolution a habit in Russia. She illustrated the same connection between tyranny as cause and conspiracy as effect, from English, Scottish and French history in the past. The fair comment is that repression leads naturally to conspiracy, that revolution by force leads to counter-revolution, whether the tyrant is called Nikolas or Stalin. Beatrice asks in so many words: 'How long is this apparently continuous series of conspiracies and attempts at counter-revolution to last?' The answer is: So long as Government cannot be changed in any other way. Democracy, as we have in Britain, may do foolish things, but at least it makes it possible and habitual to change a government without shooting it, by holding elections that are really free.

The difference between Beatrice and myself as to what I declared to be the brutality of Soviet methods flared into open controversy in the pages of the *New Statesman*. But differences of opinion never scratched the surface of our friendship. Just before this open controversy, she and Sidney had welcomed my visit to Passfield Corner with a debating team from the Ecole Libre of Paris. Just after she welcomed the School Literary Society whom Janet and I brought there.

And when *Soviet Communism* was published, I reviewed it with great kindness:

'The Webbs, I think, have made out the case for their title: Soviet Communism: A New Civilization? But not for leaving off the question mark at the end of it.'[1]

Of all the times that I spent with the Webbs over forty years, the two days of my visit to Beatrice at the Royal Bath Hotel, Bournemouth, in September 1934, while Sidney was back in Moscow, stand out in my memory, for reasons both serious and frivolous.

The serious reason is that, in those two days, I discovered more clearly than ever before the most important of all the Webb qualities. What Beatrice described to me then as her delight in still being open to new truth was something more positive than openness—it was a passion for new ideas because they were new. This quality determined the course of the

---

[1] *Political Quarterly*, July-September 1936. In a later book, after Soviet behaviour at beginning of World War II and their treatment of academic refugees whom they had taken in from Hitler, I said that the title should be all question marks. *Power and Influence*, p. 239.

Webbs again and again. It led to their embrace of Soviet Communism as something ever so much newer than outworn Socialism. It made the School of Economics, as a factory of new ideas, their favourite child. It made natural the handing over of each new-born idea to someone else to nurse; only by doing so would they have energy and time for the next adventures. It determined the character which, in the teeth of Bernard Shaw, they insisted on giving to the School—that of absolute impartiality in research and in teaching; a factory of new ideas which had prescribed for it the ideas that it might and might not pursue would be a contradiction in terms.

The frivolous reason is that I discovered at the same time what I looked like to some people. A friend of Beatrice's came into the hotel while I was there and, without knowing who I was, decided that in appearance I was 'a complex of Ariel, a Professor and a Scientist'. 'Of course I knew his fame,' she wrote to Beatrice afterwards, 'but no one had told me how wonderful he looked.' Beatrice sent me her friend's letter to keep, with a comforting re-assurance: 'She is my contemporary, so that you need not fear any further advances.' What fun Sidney and Beatrice were!

And what dears they were! I cannot end this chapter better than by citing two letters which I had from them, when my time at the School was coming to an end or ended.

The last letter of all that I had from Sidney while I was still Director of the School was a request that, in that capacity, I should invite a former benefactor of the School to give some lectures there in the coming October term. Sidney had an idea that this benefactor was now 'hard up'. He and Beatrice would themselves provide £100 to pay for the lectures. This letter was Sidney all over, remembering kindnesses for fifty years and returning them.

The letter from Beatrice came after I had moved to Oxford in the hope of finding leisure for research and writing—a hope defeated in due course by Hitler. Sidney and Beatrice had been most unwilling for me to leave the School.[1] But, now that I was in Oxford, she wrote to express her delight that I was going to have 'a splendid opportunity for carrying on the social and economic research which we all want'.

[1] See ch. VI, p. 73.

APPENDICES

1. Statistics
2. Resolutions on Political Activities
3. Notes on Illustrations

APPENDIX I

STATISTICS

This Appendix contains four tables:

A. Student Statistics for each School Session 1919-20 to 1936-7 with such comparable figures as can be given for two sessions before World War I, 1912-13 and 1913-14, and for the two latest Sessions 1956-7 and 1957-8. Provisional figures are given also for 1958-9.

B. Teacher and Income Statistics for the same Sessions.

C. School of Economics Total Income and its Percentage Sources in three Sessions between 1919 and 1937, in one Session after 1957-8, in two Sessions before World War I, and in two recent sessions 1956-7.

D. Accommodation in 1923-4, 1936-7, and 1959.

Table A: STUDENT STATISTICS 1919-37
(with figures for 1912-14 and 1956-59)

SESSION	MEN	WOMEN	TOTAL	REGULAR	INTER-COLLEGIATE	OCCASIONAL	OVERSEAS
1912-13	1,363	774	2,137		79		158
1913-14	1,354	773	2,127		94		199
1919-20	2,061	955	3,016	836	140	2,040	291
1920-21	2,231	670	2,901	978	173	1,750	354
1921-22	1,897	528	2,425	885	157	1,383	386
1922-23	1,766	609	2,375	852	167	1,356	403
1923-24	2,118	494	2,612	818	155	1,708	440
1924-25	2,193	572	2,765	849	297	1,619	484
1925-26	2,226	559	2,785	879	351	1,555	550
1926-27	2,286	585	2,871	965	367	1,539	623
1927-28	2,165	638	2,803	1,014	431	1,358	607
1928-29	2,207	601	2,808	985	408	1,415	653
1929-30	2,253	669	2,922	1,115	483	1,323	625
1930-31	2,255	682	2,937	1,233	471	1,233	582
1931-32	2,256	679	2,935	1,226	501	1,208	546
1932-33	2,229	710	2,939	1,340	481	1,118	652
1933-34	2,279	683	2,962	1,417	498	1,047	743
1934-35	2,296	733	3,029	1,385	577	1,067	719
1935-36	2,310	725	3,035	1,446	591	998	721
1936-37	2,282	718	3,000	1,439	597	964	717
1956-57	2,931	899	3,830	2,448	1,039	343	710
1957-58	2,979	885	3,864	2,529	1,000	335	942
1958-59			3,905	2,531	1,078	296	

Table B: TEACHER AND INCOME STATISTICS 1919-37
(with figures for 1912-14 and 1956-59)

SESSION	TEACHERS		INCOME £		
	FULL TIME	PART TIME	TOTAL	ENDOWMENT	FEES
1912-13	67		17,238	108	6,544
1913-14	67		17,813	108	7,140
1919-20	17	42	25,066	708	10,748
1920-21	21	31	52,233	7,168	19,238
1921-22	26	47	50,100	7,783	17,657
1922-23	27	52	52,798	9,635	17,671
1923-24	29	66	58,247	10,189	19,202
1924-25	30	59	64,408	10,513	23,089
1925-26	44	50	79,770	9,746	24,683
1926-27	43	46	82,485	10,926	26,363
1927-28	50	53	90,823	14,961	28,958
1928-29	49	51	96,460	18,033	30,843
1929-30	55	74	97,682	17,641	34,155
1930-31	57	70	115,175	16,719	34,771
1931-32	69	64	133,706	17,239	34,050
1932-33	73	49	134,263	17,790	35,443
1933-34	82	55	131,202	17,720	35,959
1934-35	76	51	131,327	17,185	36,467
1935-36	84	45	135,092	17,412	38,759
1936-37	79	44	135,014	17,452	37,538
1956-57	182	26	522,173	19,275	73,014
1957-58	182	25	629,822	19,977	102,129
1958-59					

The general movement of student numbers in the review period 1919 to 1937 is discussed in the first section of Chapter III. To what is said there, two comments only need be added:

First, the classification of students as regular or occasional respectively is made on a slightly different principle for the first four sessions, up to 1922-3 inclusive, from that used for the later sessions. But comparison of the figures before and after the change is not affected substantially. The figures of Inter-collegiate and Overseas Students are not affected at all.

Second, five of the early years of this period show exceptional distribution of student numbers by sex. In the first year of all (1919-20) there are relatively more women—one to every two men, and in the four years 1923 to 1927 there are relatively fewer women—one to every four men. The larger proportion of women in 1919-20 probably reflects an earlier return of women from war service on the Government grants. The smaller proportion of women from 1923 to 1927 may be no more than a reaction from the first year—a way back to the normal one to three, which appears, with minor differences in most of the other years of the review period and in the last two years shown in the table, from 1956 to 1958. In the two pre-war Sessions at the head of the table, 1912-13 and 1913-14, the proportion is higher, well above one woman to every two men.

The student numbers for the latest sessions 1956-8 show a rise in total, from 3,000 to over 3,800, the rise being proportionately greatest among the inter-collegiate and regular students, though substantial also with overseas students. By contrast the occasional students show a marked fall, to a little over 300 in each of these sessions as compared with nearly 1,000 twenty years before. There was still in 1956-7 a substantial body both of regular students (488) and of inter-collegiate students (89), i.e. 577 in total, taking full courses in the evening.

But, while the School today still has a substantial number of regular students in the evenings, in relation to the total of regular students they are fewer than they used to be. At the end of my Directorate in 1936-7 sixty-one per cent of the regular students came by day and thirty-nine per cent came in the evening. Twenty years after, in the session 1956-7 eighty per cent of the regular students came by day and twenty per cent in the evening. For whatever reason, the School of Economics today is more of a day school and less of an evening school for people already at work than it was twenty years ago.

The provisional figures for the last session of all 1958-9 show further rises of regular and inter-collegiate students and a further fall of occasional students.

The figures in Table B in the main speak for themselves. It is not possible to distinguish accurately between full time and part time teachers before World War I.

TABLE C

SCHOOL OF ECONOMICS TOTAL INCOME AND ITS PERCENTAGE SOURCES

Session	Total £	Total %	Fees %	Endow-ment %	Other %
1895-97	2,369	100.0	10.8	40.1	49.1
1913-14	17,813	100.0	40.0	.6	59.4
1919-20	25,066	100.0	42.9	2.8	54.3
1920-21	52,233	100.0	36.8	13.7	49.5
1936-37	135,014	100.0	27.8	12.9	59.3
1957-58	629,822	100.0	16.2	3.2	80.6

The table compares total Income of the School of Economics in a Session before the war and in the last session (1957-8) and its main sources (Fees, Endowment, Other) with corresponding figures at end of the period 1919-37.

NOTES ON TABLE C

The figures in the top row represent the mean of the first two sessions of the School, 1895-7. The percentage shown under Endowment represents 'Donations and Subscriptions' averaging £949 per year. Of the 'Other Income' (averaging £1,164 per year) nearly three-quarters (£850 per year) represents Technical Education Board Grants, and most of the rest is rent paid by the British Library of Political Science, then independent of the School. The Fees represent only a tenth of the total income; the School was only just launched and there were very few regular students.

The outstanding features of the rest of the table are:

i Growth of total income.

ii Large proportion coming from Other Sources—in the main Treasury and Local Authority Grants—and its rise in the last year to more than eighty per cent of the whole.

iii Decline of fee income, apart from the slight rise in 1919-20 representing presumably the students with grants allowed them for war service. The decline to 1957-8 is particularly marked.

iv A rise of Endowments in the period under review (1920 to 1937) which has now come to an end.

Broadly the taxpayer and the ratepayer maintain the School of Economics today, as no doubt they maintain many or most comparable institutions.

TABLE D: ACCOMMODATION IN 1923-24, 1936-37, 1959

Type of Accommodation	1923-24		1936-37		1959		
	sq. ft.	% of whole	sq. ft.	% of whole	sq. ft.	% of whole	No. of Rooms
Lecture and Classrooms	17,970	35.2	21,374	16.0	22,085	11.7	33
Teachers' Rooms	4,190	8.2	17,612	13.2	21,132	11.2	167
Social Rooms	10,540	20.6	23,479	17.4	37,173	19.7	27
Library and Seminar (Study) Rooms	7,585	14.9	38,400	28.7	47,161	24.9	
Administration	2,300	4.5	5,483	4.1	9,429	5.0	
Circulation	8,500	16.6	27,412	20.6	38,613	20.5	
New Categories— Research Staff					6,861	3.6	39
Departmental Clerical and Secretarial Staff					3,987	2.1	
Technical Accommodation*					2,448	1.3	
Total	51,085	100.0	133,760	100.0	188,889	100.0	

* Laboratories, Machine Rooms, Photostats, etc.

NOTES ON TABLE D — ACCOMMODATION

Comparing the earliest figures (1923-4) with the latest (1959) Table D shows that the proportionate space used as Lecture and Classroom has fallen to a third (from 35.2 to 11.7 per cent of the whole) while Library and Seminar Rooms have increased substantially and Teachers' Rooms appreciably, as has Circulation. Social Rooms and Administration occupy much the same proportion now as at the beginning.

If the new categories are added to the old categories to which they appear nearest, putting Research Staff and Technical Accommodation with Library and Seminar Rooms increases substantially the proportion of this latter, and Departmental Clerical and Secretarial Staff adds something to Administration.

APPENDIX II

RESOLUTIONS ON STAFF AND POLITICAL ACTIVITIES

The Resolutions set out below were approved on May 19, 1932 on the recommendation of the Emergency Committee, as agreed by the Professorial Council.

(1) That while members of the staff of the School of Economics should, in the full sense secured to them by Article 28 of the Memorandum and Articles of Association of the School, be free from regulation or censure by the Governors of the School in respect of their writings of public speeches, they should regard it as a personal duty to preserve in such writings or speeches a proper regard for the reputation of the School as an academic centre of scientific teaching and research.

(2) That any member of the regular staff contemplating becoming a candidate or prospective candidate for Parliament should be asked to inform the Director of this at the earliest possible moment, and in the prosecution of his candidature, if occasion arises, should make it clear that the School itself embraces members of different political parties and has no political affiliation.

(3) That subject to the requirements of the School, limited leave of absence without pay may from time to time be granted by the Director from official duties to candidates during an election campaign.

(4) That the position of members of the regular staff (whether full time or part time) becoming Members of the House of Commons should be considered, after reports from the Appointments Committee, in each case on the merits, subject to the principle that, as a general rule, membership of the House of Commons is inconsistent with the tenure of a full time post at the School.

(5) That the School should be free to continue to associate with its work as special lecturers and honorary members of the Common Room those who have served it on the regular staff, but have ceased to be members for any of the reasons indicated above.

APPENDICES

[Note: The Professorial Council have been informed by the Director that:

(a) On Resolution 5 the Committee had no intention of debarring a person who had abandoned an active political career from applying thereafter for a vacant position on the staff of the School.

(b) On Resolution 1 it was the intention of the Committee that the Director would be expected to make a 'light intervention' in cases of infringement.

(c) On Resolution 4 in the case of teachers appointed by the University and over whose appointments the School had no immediate control, it was intended that these resolutions could be taken as indicating the tenor of the report of the Governors to the Senate of the University.]

RESOLVED: That the Resolutions as finally agreed by the Emergency Committee and the Professorial Council be accepted and that they be forwarded to all present members of the staff and to all new members of staff upon their taking up their appointments.

ARTICLE 28 OF THE ARTICLES OF ASSOCIATION (JUNE 1901)

28 No religious, political or economic test or qualification shall be made a condition for or disqualify from receiving any of the benefits of the Corporation, or holding any office therein; and no member of the Corporation, or professor, lecturer or other officer thereof, shall be under any disability or disadvantage by reason only of any opinions that he may hold or promulgate on any subject whatsoever.

APPENDIX III

NOTES ON SOME OF THE ILLUSTRATIONS

Rag of May 28, 1920, facing page 17

The central figure represents Sir Walter Raleigh borrowed regularly for such occasions. The student in front carrying the broom is William Ewart Green who came to the School after war service in the Field Artillery and went on to work in the London and North Eastern Railway and other transport jobs. On his left is Alan T. Davis, President of the Students' Union in 1920-21 and on his right a little behind is F. J. Copelin then and to this day 39 years later still on the Library staff. Behind Green, with mortar board, is George Grant McKenzie who after five years' war service took the B.Sc.Econ. went on to research for the Union of Post Office Workers and later for the Labour Party. Behind him on the right of Raleigh are S. H. Cair later in the Extra Mural Department of the University of Bristol, F. Waldo Forge later City Editor of the *Glasgow Herald*, and W. F. Crick who became manager of Intelligence in the Midland Bank; on Raleigh's left are R. H. Kastell who went on to collection of Economic and Parliamentary information, and W. J. G. Willis who came to the School after five years' war service and after a short business job, went to the Library and Information Department of the Conservative Central Office.

The particulars given here are taken from the Register of the School 1895-1932 and may not be up to date. But they illustrate the great variety of careers undertaken from the School.

Janet and her Four Children, facing page 16

Janet is just outside Buckingham Palace on return from receiving the O.B.E. in 1918. The British Empire Order had only just been created, and she was one of the first women to receive the O.B.E. for service which was in no sense women's work, but in effect released a man for war service. For the Ministry of Food she was in charge of distribution of all the bacon bought by it.

The children from Janet's right are:

Lucy Philip, now Dr. Mair and Reader in Social Anthropology in the London School of Economics.

Elizabeth Christian (Elspeth), who managed the Master's Lodgings at University College for me for two years, till she married

Richard Stanley Burn, a former member of the college (and son of one of its benefactors), who came to see me there.

Philip Beveridge Mair, now in charge of the factories of C.I.B.A. (Chemical Industries of Basle) at Horsham and Grimsby.

Ethel Marjory Beveridge, now Mrs R. Ll. Gwilt of Edinburgh, and herself mother of four children most of whom have become musicians, and one of whom played a Bach Aria at the Memorial Service to Janet.

Army Class, facing page 33

The sending of the pre-war Army Class to the School in 1908 has been recorded in *An Epic of Clare Market*. It was a great pleasure to Janet and myself to welcome the return of an Army Class in 1924, but alas in 1932 they fell victims to depression economy by H.M. Treasury. The Class are seated in front of the front door forming part of the 1920-22 building.

Visitors to Green Street, Avebury, facing page 48

Arnold Plant and Lionel Robbins both have a double claim to appear in the gallery of my period, as having been there both as students for the whole of their courses, and as Professors. Arnold Plant was President of the Students Union and deserves thanks for having identified practically all the raggers of May 1920. Lionel Robbins, in taking the title of Lord Robbins of Clare Market has recalled his happy days at L.S.E.

Visitors to Green Street, Avebury, facing page 49

Graham Wallas, Fabian Ware (under whom author worked on the *Morning Post*), André Siegfried and Harry and Jeanette Tawney.

Staff v. Students match, facing page 80

On the Director's left is Mrs. Anstey, standing behind her Professor Sargent, and to his left Baron Meyendorff, described on p. 61.

INDEX

Aberdeen 92

Academic Assistance Council 49

Akbar 71

Alperton 59

American Educational Mission 17

Annual Digest of Public International Law 51

Annual Survey of English Law 51

Anstey, Mrs. Vera 61, 128

Anthony, Miss 66, 72

Ashfield, Lord 60

Asquith, H. H. 36, 52, 70

Astor, Viscountess 64

Attlee, Clement 58

Austen, Jane 37

Australia 17, 22

Austria 68

Babur 71

Baldwin, Stanley (Prime Minister) 66

Balliol College 33, 35, 39, 75, 76, 109

Barker, W. R. 24

Berry, Sir William 24, 26

Beveridge, Henry 67, 71, 72

Beveridge, Mrs. Henry (author's mother) 37, 41, 65, 66, 67, 69, 70, 71, 72, 73, 74, 76

Beveridge, the Lady—her *An Epic of Clare Market* is ante-cedent of this book 7; which includes record of her activities at L.S.E. 8; appointed secretary 20, 21; interviewed by Sir William M'Cormick 22; asks L.C.C. for help on Houghton Street site 26; crosswords 28; 'Sixty Years On' in *Clare Market Review* 29; memories of St. Andrews colours approach to students 33; Students Union Executive entertained 36; inaugurates Lunch Hour Concerts 37; inaugurates Literary Society 37-8; Green Street 40; election of new students 41; graduates' appreciation 42-3, 45; teachers' conditions improved 46-8; appreciation of Professor Cannan and Professor Knowles 49; acquisition of Malden field 59-60; Inter-Allied Commission to Vienna 68; vacation activities 70, 74; help with parents 71-2; function of administrative staff 82; talks with Beardsley Ruml 85, 94; urges modern language teaching 86; suggests Civil Service Course 87; retires as Secretary 1937 96; discusses Beatrice Webb's handwriting 106; takes Literary Society to Passfield Corner 112; illustration described 127-8

I

Beveridge, Lord (author) — scope of book 7-8; acknowledgements 9; invited to become Director, May 1919 15; jobs then waiting to be done at L.S.E. 16; buildings inadequate 18; staff inadequate 19; existing staff 19, 20; Mrs. Mair appointed Secretary 20; Miss MacTaggart retires 21; dealings with University Grants Committee 22; new building scheme 23-8; full University life for students envisaged 33-4; students' extra-curricular activities 35, 37-9; students' vacation activities 39-40; election of new students 41; appointments for graduates 42; discipline 43-44; teachers' salaries reorganised 46-7; and general conditions improved 48; aid to German teachers 49; teachers' publications 50-51; leave of absence for research 51; not a politician 52-3; School's impartiality questioned 53; and proved 54-6; Oration, 1937 56-8, 94-5; athletics field acquired 59; games at Houghton Street 60; field sports 60-61; 'Felix' 61-2; criminal at first Mock Trial 64; prosecutes in other Mock Trials 64; publications 65; Coal Commission 65-7; domestic problems 66; Civil Service claims 67-8; Unemployment Insurance Statutory Committee 68-9; full social life 69-70; care of

parents 71-3; vacation activities 74-6; International Price History 76-7; administration in 1919 78; teachers' responsibility increased 79; Governors' responsibility increased 80; academic self government sought 81-2; proposals for Natural Bases of Social Science 87-90; supported by Professorial Council, financed by Laura Spelman Fund 91; Social Biology started but abandoned 92-3; this deplored 94; retires as Director 1937 96; gives Webb Centenary Lecture 1959 97; debt to Webbs 98-113

Beveridge Report 37, 98

Blackett, Basil 68

Blair, Sir Robert 24

Bleak House, Charles Dickens 29

Booth, Charles 51, 105

Booth, Mrs. Charles 51

Booth, George 51

Boothby, Cumberland 52

Boothby, Robert 64

Bothie of Tober-na Vuolich, A. R. Clough 76

Bournemouth 112

Bowley, Professor A. L. 8, 46, 48, 49, 78n, 92, 103

Bradbury, John 68

British Association for the Advancement of Science 25, 68, 74, 84

British Food Control, W. H. Beveridge 65, 74

Brown, Valentine 24

Cair, S. H. 127
Call Back Yesterday, H. Dalton 84n
Callander, Perthshire 70, 74, 85
Cambridge 20, 22, 64, 81, 95
Candida, G. B. Shaw 40
Cannan, Professor E. 19, 20, 48, 49, 78n, 84, 85
Cassel, Sir Ernest 16
Cassel Trust 16, 83, 87n
Cave, Lord 36
Chamberlain, Joseph 105
Charterhouse 93
Churchill, Winston 36
Clare Market Review 7, 21n, 29, 33, 48, 59
Clough, A. H. 39
Cobden, Richard 16, 39
Cobden Library 39
Copelin, F. J. 127
Crick, W. F. 127
Czechoslovakia 68

Daily Herald 48, 55, 56
Dalry, Kircudbrightshire 74, 76
Dalton, Dr. H. 20, 42, 58, 84
d'Aranyi, Miss Jelly 37
Davis, A. T. 127
Defence of Free Learning, A, Lord Beveridge 68n
de la Mare, Walter 37
Delisle Burns 53
Diaries, Beatrice Webb 100 and n, 101 and n, 103n (?), 104 and n, 108, 110n
Dickens, Charles 29

Dicksee, Professor L. 19, 62
Dinnet, Aberdeenshire 72, 75, 76
Dobson 47
Dunford House, Midhurst 16, 39, 40, 69
Durham county 20

Ecole Libre, Paris 112
Economica 50
Edinburgh 15
Einstein, A. 94, 95
Elliott, Captain, M.P. 69
Encyclopaedia Britannica 69
Epic of Clare Market, An, Lady Beveridge 7, 18n, 106, 109n, 128

Fabians 40, 104, 105, 108, 110
Fawcett, Miss Philippa 22
Financial Times 25
Forge, F. W. 127
Fosdick, Raymond 91
Founders, see Beatrice and Sidney Webb
Fox, Ruth (Mrs. H. Dalton) 20
Foxwell, Professor H. S. 18, 19 84, 103
France 51
Fulton, John 72, 75

Gater, Sir George 24
General Theory of Employment Interest and Money, M. Keynes 94
German teachers 49
Germany 51
Glover, T. R. 64

Government Departments:
Civil Service 15, 52, 53, 67, 68, 73, 87
Civil Service Commission 21n
Coal Mines, Royal Commission on 15, 65, 66, 67, 68, 72, 90
Colonial Office 109
Commonwealth Fund 86
Education, Board of 26, 28, 36
Empire Marketing Board 86
Food, Ministry of 20
House of Commons 84n, 125; Prince Consort Act 18; Private Bills Committee 25, 28; Education Bill 1902 107
House of Lords 15, 57
India Office 71
King Edward's Hospital Fund 63
Labour Exchanges 110
Local Government Committee 104
London Transport 60
National Health Service 38
Poor Law, Royal Commission on 99, 103, 104, 108, 110
Rationing Machinery, Advisory Committee on 69
Reconstruction Committee 104, 105
Tariff Policy, Commission on 67
Trade, Board of 67
Unemployment Insurance Statutory Committee 68, 104

University Grants Committee, Treasury 22, 23, 121
Graham Little, Sir Ernest 16n, 53
Green, W. E. 127
Green Street, Avebury 40, 43, 128
Gregory, Professor T. 18, 20, 64
Gutteridge, Professor H. C. 62, 84

Haldane, Dowager Lady 70, 74
Haldane, Lord 16, 23, 70, 74, 99
Hale, Cheshire 72
Halifax, Earl of 36
Hall, Hubert 76, 77
Hamilton, Lord George 104
Haslemere, Surrey 71, 72
Headicar, B. M. 17
Helvellyn, Cumberland 73
Henderson, Hubert 64
Hewins 105, 107
Highway, The, H. Sidgwick 102n
History of Trade Unionism, S. and B. Webb 108
Hitler, Adolf 49, 94, 112n, 113
Hobhouse, Professor 19, 48n, 79, 91, 92, 93
Hogben, Professor L. 92, 109
Holborn Estate School 27
Holland 51
Highes, G. P. 61
Hunt, Frank 24, 26
Hurd, Joseph 47
Hutchinson Bequest 106
Huxley, T. H. 93

Hypereides 64

India 67, 68, 71
Insull, Samuel 91
International Price History 51, 76, 77
Irvine (Everest) 70
Italy 22

Jenks, Professor E. 84
John and Irene, W. H. Beveridge 104
Jye 60

Kastell, R. H. 127
Keynes, Maynard 84, 94, 95
King George V 23, 63
King James I 28
Kingsley Martin 53
Knowles, Professor Lilian 19, 46n, 48, 49, 78n

Labour and the New Social Order, S. and B. Webb 99
Labour Party 53, 99, 104
Langdale, Cumberland 74
Laski, Professor H. 48, 53, 55, 56, 92
Laura Spelman Rockefeller Memorial 24, 25, 84, 90, 91
Law Society 84
Lee, Kenneth 72
Lees-Smith, Professor 19, 69
Liberal Summer School 52
Liverpool 68, 74, 84
Llewellyn-Smith, Sir Hubert 51, 67
Lloyd, 53
Lloyd George, David 52, 70

Lloyd George, Gwilym 64
London and Cambridge Economic Service 51
London:
    Adelphi Terrace 107
    British Museum 71
    Bush House 18
    Campden Hill 49, 59, 71
    Campden House Road 65, 67, 71
    Clare Market 23, 26, 28, 29, 49
    Exhibition Road 63
    Gower Street 63
    Highgate 69
    John Street 107
    Mansion House 36
    St. Clement's Press 24, 25, 26
    Stepney 41
    Strand, the 63
    Whitechapel 105
    Wimbledon 69
London County Council 22, 23, 24, 25, 28
    Technical Education Board 32, 109, 121
London Mercury 37
London School of Economics—birth 7; first visit to 8; Webb Centenary Lecture 8, 97-113; acknowledgements 9; author asked to become Director 15, 17; Commerce degree founded 15, 16; Cassel Trust fund 16; number of students 8, 16, 17, 18, 30-33, 118, 120; new building 16, 18, 23; library built 18; Senior Common Room 18, 125; staff increased 19; administration by Council and Committee 19, 79-82;

growth necessitates increased administration 21; University Grants 22; Houghton Street building 23-28, 33, 53, 60, 84n, 85, 90, 92; Founders' Room 27, 97, 108; necessity for remaining on original site 28; student activities 33-45, 96; Students Union 7, 21, 33, 34, 35, 36, 38, 39, 61, 62, 82; Oration Day 35, 37, 56; Commemoration Week 35, 36, 37, 94; Director's Prize 35; Literary Society 37, 38, 43, 112; Commerce Society 38; Lunch Hour Concerts 37; scholarships 40-42; appointments 42-3; refectory 44; Mock Trials 47, 61, 63, 64; 'Felix' 61, 62, 63; teachers' salaries and emoluments 46-8, 119, 120; aid to German teachers 49; research encouraged 50; publications 50-51; Labour adherents among staff 53; but School impartial 54; and teachers should remain so 56-8; athletics at Alperton 59; Malden sports ground 35, 59, 60, 61, 84n; eight presented 59; transport to Malden 60; games at Houghton Street 60; administration under Miss MacTaggart 78; reorganisation of administration 79; subjects taught 83; widening of scope 83-94; but not wide enough 95; debt to Webbs 97-113

Administration — Advisers of Studies 34, 35; Annual Reports 35, 36, 37, 38, 42, 44, 60, 61, 96; Appoint-ments Committee 79, 80, 82, 125; Appointments Officer 42; Board of Discipline 80; Calendars 17, 21, 42, 50, 61, 69; Emergency Committee 44, 54, 55, 56, 79, 82, 87, 93, 125, 126; Governors 22, 54, 78, 79, 80, 82, 93, 101; Library Committee 79; Office Committee 19, 79; Professorial Council 19, 49, 54, 55, 56, 58, 78, 79, 80, 81, 82, 87, 91, 92, 94, 125, 126

Lowell (Principal of Harvard) 53
Lowes-Dickinson 19
Lynd, Mrs. Robert 70

M'Cormick, Sir William 22, 39
MacDonald, Ramsay 109
McKenzie, G. G. 127
Mackinder, Sir Halford 19, 65, 105, 108
McNair, Professor A. 92
MacTaggart, Miss 17, 21, 22, 78
Maggs, C. E. 62
Mair, D. B. 7, 20, 21n, 22, 70
Mair, Jessy, see Lady Beveridge
Mair, P. B. 74, 91
Malinowski, Professor B. 92
Mallory (Everest) 70
Man's Place in Nature, T. H. Huxley 93
Mantoux 19
Marshall 95
Marx, Karl 95
Maxton, James 64

Meteorology 71

Meyendorff, Baron 61, 128

Mitchell, Wesley 40

Miller, Eric 59

Money — Commerce degree provides 7; Cassel Trust 16, 87n; Commerce degree appeal 16, fund 23, 24; Librarian's salary 16; University Grants Committee 22, 23; grants for building in Houghton Street 23, 24, 25, 26; evening study prerequisite for L.C.C. grant 32-3; entrance scholarships 41; staff salaries 46-8, 55-6; education allowances 46-7; group pensions scheme 47; gifts for playing field and eight 59; raised for King Edward's Hospital Fund —; Director's salary cut as Chairman of Government Committee 68; Laura Spelman grants 85, 91; Commonwealth Fund grant 86; Empire Marketing Board grant 86; Business Administration grant 86; gives Webbs freedom 102; Webbs supply lecturer's fee 113; statistical table 121

Monro, Harold 37

Moscow 110, 111, 112

Murray, Professor Gilbert 52

Mussolini, Benito 94

My Apprenticeship, Beatrice Webb 100

Natural Bases of Social Science 85, 87, 88, 91, 94

Natural Selection, Wallace 93

New Machiavelli, H. G. Wells 101

New Statesmen 99, 104, 108, 110, 112

New Survey of London Life and Labour 51, 92

Nicholson, J. S. 69

Nikolas, Tsar 112

North, Christopher 28

Oriel, Provost of 52

Origin of Species, Charles Darwin 93

Our Partnership, Beatrice Webb 100, 107 and n, 108, 110n

Oxford 64, 77, 80, 81, 93, 113

Oxford Dictionary of Quotations 28

Panormo, George 47

Passfield Corner, Hampshire 99, 112

Passfield Trustees 9

Passmore Edwards 18

Passmore Edwards Hall 28

Peace in Austria 68

Pearce Higgins 19

Philip, William 22

Pick, Sir Frank 60

Pitfold, Hampshire 40, 65, 67, 71, 72

Plant, Professor A. 128

Plato 64

Politica 51, 56n, 94n

Political Quarterly 112n

Population and Unemployment 84

Power and Influence, Lord Beveridge 8, 48n, 51n, 52, 55n, 56n, 61n, 63n, 67n, 73n, 74, 99n, 101n, 105n, 112n

Prince of Wales 37

Public Finance 42

Queen Anne 28

Raleigh, Sir Walter 127

Rathbone, Miss Eleanor 46

Red Lion 21n, 23

Reeves, Pember 15, 21

Review of Activities 27

Ricardo 95

Robbins, Professor L. (Lord Robbins) 49, 128

Robson 53

Rockefeller, John D. 84n

Rockefeller Foundation 27, 51, 84n

Rogers, Thorold 76

Ruml, Beardsley 24, 84, 85, 87, 88, 90, 94

Russell-Wells, Sir Sydney 15, 16, 23

Russia 110, 111, 112

Russian ballet 69

St. Andrews 22, 23

Salter, Sir Arthur 64, 73

Sankey, Lord 87n

Sargent, Professor A. J. 19, 46, 78n, 128

Savill, Dr Agnes 69

Seligman, Professor 19, 48n

Shaw, George Bernard 40, 101, 106, 113

Sidgwick, Hugh 101

Siegfried, André 40, 128

Social Insurance Bill 52, 53, 70

Sokolnikov 111

Soviet Communism 103, 106, 110, 111, 112, 113

Spender, J. A. 64

Spurgeon, Dr Caroline 37

Stalin 112

Stamp, Sir Josiah 46, 56

Stephenson, Professor W. T. 19

Steel-Maitland, Sir Arthur 25n

Stopes, Dr Marie 84

Student Vanguard 43

Subjects:
  Anthropology and Colonial Administration 50, 89, 92
  Economics—
    Banking and Currency 50
    Accounting 50
    Commerce 7, 15, 19, 20, 24, 36, 42, 50, 52, 86, 87n
    Business Administration 86
    Civil Service Course 87
    Economic Psychology 89
    Geography 50
  History, 19, 49, 50
    Imperial Economic Relations 86
    International Studies 50, 92
    Law 50, 83
    Mental Health 86
    Modern Languages 16, 50, 86, 87n
    Political Science 50, 55
    Psychology 50
    Public Health 89
    Social Biology 24, 50, 81, 89, 92, 93, 109
    Sociology 50

Statistics 19, 50
Transport 50
Russian Institutions and Economics 61
Political Economy 85
Sweden, Crown Prince of 66

Tawney, Jeanette 128
Tawney, Professor H. 53, 128
Tibetan Lamas 70
Times, The 66
Toronto 25, 68
Trade Cycle 44
Trevelyan, Sir Charles 24
Trevelyan, Mr and Mrs G. M. 74

Unemployment—A Problem of Industry, W. H. Beveridge 65, 72, 75, 76
United States of America 25, 37, 43, 44, 67, 91, 109
    Harvard 51, 53, 91
    New York 85
    Pekin, Illinois 91
University of London 8, 15, 22, 61, 70, 82, 84, 99
    Academic Council 81
    Bloomsbury Site 8, 25, 28, 60, 72
    Imperial College 99
    King's College 31, 84, 86
    National Institute of Industrial Psychology 89
    Senate 15, 25, 26, 27, 28, 80
    Vice Chancellorship 90
Urwick 19

Varia Beveridge 65
Vienna 49, 68
Virgil 63

Wakefield, Russell 103
Wales 74
Wallace, John 64
Wallas, Professor Graham 19, 40, 48n, 53, 55, 128
Ware, Sir Fabian 128
Webbs and their Work, The 101n
Webb, Beatrice — Centenary lecture 8-9, 97-113; attends Students Union executive dinner 36; visits Green Street 40; research needs money 46; research as important as teaching 50-51; employed on Booth survey 51; no limit to ambitions for L.S.E. 83; scientific methods desired for economic studies 94, 95
Webb, Sidney—Centenary lecture 8-9, 97-113; asks author to become Director 15, 17, 23, 52, 65, 67; puts current L.S.E. problems 16; builds Passmore Edwards Hall 28; makes evening study condition of giving money 32; comments on research at Students Union dinner 36; receives Pitfold prospectus from author 39; visits Green Street 40; research needs money 46; research as important as teaching 50-51, 81; did not meet Beatrice till after Booth survey 51; no limit to ambitions for L.S.E. 83; meets Beardsley Ruml 84; chooses Hogben as Professor of Social Biology 92; scientific methods desired for economic studies 94, 95; says that by 1937

L.S.E. 're-founded' 96; un-
selfishness 97
Westermark 19, 48n
Williams, S. A. 37
Willis, W. J. G. 127
Wilson Potter, J. 24, 25n
Wilson, Walter 47
Wolf, Professor 19, 91

Woods, Col Arthur 84n
Woolf, Leonard 53
Wordsworth, William 28
World War I 8, 61, 104
World War II 8

Young, Professor Allyn 91

Printed in the United States
by Baker & Taylor Publisher Services